The Art of
Online Dating

Alyssa Dineen

Founder of Style My Profile

The Art of *Online* Dating

Style Your Most Authentic Self and Cultivate a Mindful Dating Life

HARPER HORIZON

Published by Harper Horizon, an imprint of HarperCollins Focus LLC.

Book design by Aubrey Khan, Neuwirth & Associates.

Any internet addresses, phone numbers, or company or product information printed in this book are offered as a resource and are not intended in any way to be or to imply an endorsement by Harper Horizon, nor does Harper Horizon vouch for the existence, content, or services of these sites, phone numbers, companies, or products beyond the life of this book.

Names and identifying characteristics of some individuals have been changed to preserve their privacy.

ISBN 978-0-7852-4172-0 (eBook)
ISBN 978-0-7852-4171-3 (HC)

Library of Congress Control Number: 2021936698

Printed in the United States of America
21 22 23 24 25 LSC 10 9 8 7 6 5 4 3 2 1

For Hayden & Story

Contents

Foreword

What you wear and how you present yourself is a true calling card to the world around you. Caring for your appearance in an authentic way shows real confidence and makes you feel empowered. Alyssa Dineen is the perfect Style Guru for all who might be lost as to how they can best showcase themselves.

I have known Alyssa for many years, as a colleague and a friend. I have seen her transform men and women in such a brilliant way that never feels intimidating but makes them feel safe and cared for, which then boosts their self-esteem to new levels.

As a divorced woman who has also been in the world of online dating, I immediately recognized the brilliance of starting a business to help others with their dating profiles. I know her clients feel like they're working with a friend who has been through it and, after seeing thousands of other people's profiles, knows what works and what doesn't.

Her gentle yet effective approach brings out the best in everyone she touches, which speaks volumes not only to her character but also to her limitless talent. She has a magic of understanding each individual and what works best for their unique personality and lifestyle.

I also watched as Alyssa transformed herself, both physically and emotionally, after leaving an oppressive marriage. I observed how she tried new makeup techniques, wore her hair in various styles, and experimented with looks for dating and for work. After some trial and error, she found her true style—and her true self. I watched as Alyssa blossomed and became who she is today: a confident woman and successful business owner who met the partner she deserves.

I hope that you, too, will be inspired by her journey and learn from her hard-earned wisdom!

Carmindy Bowyer

beauty enabler, makeup artist, author,
speaker, host, and founder of Carmindy Beauty

Dear Reader

Cheers to you! Deciding to jump into online dating is a great step in moving forward with whatever new stage you're entering in life. For me, it was divorce—after eighteen years together, including eleven years married—that pushed me into the unknowns of being a single mother of two at the age of forty-one.

Whatever brings you to this book, I hope you'll find a practical guide to the world of online dating, pep talks to keep you going, and the knowledge that you are not alone. I'll share some of my personal dating stories with you—some that make me cringe, some that make me smile, and some that make me spit out my coffee laughing. I'd say "I've seen it all," but every time I do, something surprises me. Online dating can be mysterious and frustrating at times, but it can also be fun and fulfilling. It's always an opportunity for learning more about yourself, and it truly can lead to long-term romantic partnerships and friendships.

As a professional stylist and art director for photo shoots, I figured out the art of creating an engaging profile quicker than most. In fact, I got to be so good at it and felt such a passion for helping other people through the process, I started a business to help singles in all stages of life create a successful online dating presence—from fashion to photo to bio to learning how to communicate via dating apps—so they can make the best experience for themselves. I've divided this book into five chapters, to put all this information in one place.

Chapter 1: Rediscover Your Style—and Your Self. Before I was ready to distill myself and my style into a few profile pics and bio sentences, I needed to remember who that person was and what she thought, felt, and liked to do. I had to get to know myself and my style all over again. If you feel the same way, I'll walk you through the steps I found helpful in rediscovering myself and helping my clients do the same.

Chapter 2: Style Your Look. I'll help you create a new wardrobe for your new self. It doesn't have to break the bank—I'll share the fifteen essentials every woman needs in her closet and a guide to creating your FDU, or first-date uniform. You'll never be trying on your whole closet searching for that perfect outfit, since you'll have it ready. One less thing to worry about.

Chapter 3: Style Your Bio. Photos get all the buzz when it comes to online profiles, but what really elevates the process from a "meet" market to more personalized matches that will lead to better dates is a good bio. I'll help you craft one that will attract the right kind of matches for you.

Chapter 4: Style Your Selfie. If you're like me, even with my experience on fashion shoots, being on the other side of the camera is torture—at first. This chapter has lots of practical tips on taking selfies, getting better photos of yourself, and choosing which photos to post on your profile.

Chapter 5: Style Your Swiping. Here's where all your hard work and prep blossom into an art. I'll give you the low-down on the most popular apps and how they work and the language of online messaging, communication by text, and how to navigate those first IRL (in real life) dates. And how to keep swiping until, like me, you find what you've been looking for.

I hope you'll find this book helpful. I wrote it because I wish I'd had it when I was starting on this wild and rewarding journey. So dig in, grab a friend for help when you need it, and keep swiping.

Happy dating!

Alyssa

The Art of
Online Dating

1

Rediscover Your Style—and Your Self

Facing My Closet

I stood in front of my new, much smaller full-length mirror inside my new, much smaller closet, in my new, much smaller walk-up apartment. I wanted to move or fall to my knees and weep. Even a wail of agony would have been welcome. But I was immobile. I stood in my droopy, lifeless gray sweater and realized: *None of this is me.* This closet, this apartment, this sweater—nothing was familiar. I was a stranger to my own closet, my home, myself. Though I knew none of this was who I was, what I didn't know was: What was me?

How the hell did I get to this closet moment at the age of forty-one? That's a long story. So, let me start with my clothes. My clothes! Only a few days earlier, I'd unpacked two wardrobe boxes, three giant duffle bags, and two enormous, ripped garbage bags. That was it: my autobiography of cotton and denim and silk and wool. As a stylist—someone who has made a living out of choosing what looks best on that person at that time in that place—clothing has always been inextricably linked to my identity. But in that closet, I noticed something for the first time, the most obvious thing in the world. How had I never seen it before?

Nowhere in those racks and piles was *me*. The black twill pants my ex-husband loved on me that were so tight and hard to zip up that I winced just looking at them. The weird, sculptural necklace my ex-husband bought for me that looked like something a great-aunt would have left me when she died. The oversized muumuus that were "perfect for summer" . . . if I were a retiree in Palm Beach. The boring black dress—if a square and a blob had a baby, it would be more interesting. I'd bought it simply because "it fit" after I had my second baby and my husband was invited to an industry event. And the red stilettos (yes, *that* cliché) that I bought out of desperation to spice things up with my then-husband. Not me. Not me. And definitely not me. Suddenly, my entire closet: not me. And that gray sweater I was wearing? The most not me of all. My clothes had abruptly become a microcosm of the life I'd escaped.

On one side, sad and mom-ish and boring. The wardrobe of defeat. And on the other side, the "trying to be something I'm not" things my husband liked me to wear, or that I felt I should wear to look more professional with clients. Nowhere was me.

In the end, I did fall on the floor and cry.

So, what does a woman sobbing on the floor of her closet have to do with online dating and styling advice? A lot, actually.

As I lay in a heap on the floor, the world's tiniest light bulb went off above my head. That was the moment I realized that postdivorce was also self-discovery. That was day one, minute one, of my new life—the life of figuring out what made me feel good in my own skin. That was the moment that led to this book. Because if I can pull myself out of my heap, if I can understand where style and personality and online dating intersect, then maybe the future isn't so grim. And maybe there is value in that for someone else.

Online dating, I would learn, is its own special kind of beast. What I wouldn't give for someone to have shown me the road map. That's what this book is: a guide, a user's manual to online dating—the good, the bad, and the virtual flashers (oh, yes). The stuff that no one is ever going to tell you, until now. You know what else they won't tell you? That you need to lean into it. (Maybe not the flashers.) But you need to commit to that world, no matter how crazy you think it is. That's how you start to feel confident and happy and good and, most of all, like yourself again. Yes, you need the right positive attitude, but try telling that to the person in a heap on the floor. It's not an easy path, but it's a rewarding one.

This is my solemn pledge to you: I will tell you the things I wish I'd known. I will tell you about the crazies and the craziness. I will tell you about the lows and the lowers. I will tell you about the clothes that saw me through it all, what worked for me, what betrayed me, what I learned from each piece. I will tell you how I leaned on my friends, how I would feel so paralyzed during and after my divorce (i.e., during and after my closet breakdown) that I'd have to call a friend to tell me what to make for dinner.

I'll share what I learned not only by going through it myself, but also as I run a business dedicated to helping single people rediscover themselves and their style, so they can put themselves out into the dating world with newfound confidence and a kick-ass dating profile. I've learned that while the process can be painful at times, it can also be liberating, empowering, and even fun.

That woman on her closet floor, with no future and no hope, is still part of me. But now, she's also a teacher. She showed me the way forward. She showed me how to make small changes feel big. And that the only way out is *through*.

Why am I qualified to help other women through? As a New York City stylist for more than twenty years, I have not only worked with celebrities and models on fashion magazine shoots and commercials, but also with real women like me, who have complicated body issues, insecurities, and who simply don't have enough time to devote to their wardrobe. Women who are overworked, overwhelmed, or flat-out hate shopping.

I stumbled on my career in the first place because my boyfriend, whom I'd met when I graduated college, was a photographer. I'd tried a couple of different jobs, including in social work and interior design, that didn't feel right at the time. I'd recently quit an administrative assistant job and was aimlessly looking for my path in life. As a way to make some money while I was figuring it out, I started assisting some of the stylists my boyfriend worked with. I liked being on set and meeting new people all the time. I had always been into clothes but had never considered it as a career.

Before I knew it, I was styling my own shoots and building my career as a fashion stylist. And the photographer boyfriend had become my fiancé and then my husband. I worked for magazines and on advertising jobs. A few up-and-coming celebrities asked me to style them on a regular basis, which eventually led to working with private clients. I liked working one-on-one with people and helping them through their sometimes complex relationships with clothes, including the psychology of how people look, how they see themselves, and even the financial aspect of it all. I always said the job was part therapy and part fashion. I felt like my degree in psychology was finally being put to good use.

I'd been working with personal clients for about seven years when I left my marriage and started online dating. And that's when I had to start styling *myself*—which was way more daunting than it should have been for a New York City stylist.

Back to my closet. Listen, I know I'm not the first woman to cry on her floor postdivorce. I'm probably one of thousands, if not millions. And please don't get me wrong—I wasn't sad because I was alone in a new apartment after eighteen-plus years of being partnered. I was sad because I didn't know who I was anymore. In trying to keep my spouse happy, I had lost sight of myself. It occurred to me in that moment—standing in my prewar, paint-peeling storage closet with the shredded wall-to-wall carpet, which I'd tried to turn into a feminine "dressing room" with a white, fluffy IKEA rug and a white-cushioned stool—that I didn't have to keep anything in that closet. I wasn't going to start walking around naked and I had real financial considerations, but I could trash the whole thing and start fresh.

I started by inviting over my best friend, who's also a stylist, to help me purge my closet. My new closet would no longer be the closet of a "mother of two." It would now be the closet of a single woman starting over. Armed with a bottle of wine, two glasses, and a giant trash bag, we got to work.

In my decades of being a stylist, I've been on the other side of this process more times than I can count. But it was foreign to have the focus on me. As we pared down further and further, the act felt liberating. I had so many things in my wardrobe that didn't work for my new life. I threw them into the giveaway pile with zero regrets.

During this process, I also realized I desperately needed to buy some items for my new life, specifically my dating life. Buying things for myself had become an anxiety trigger. I had a hard time doing it, which was part of the reason I owned a bunch of things that weren't truly me. My wardrobe consisted of things leftover from photo shoots, things my ex had bought for me, and things I'd bought on impulse when I was pressured to buy something for an important meeting or a party, such as the boring black dress.

Why did I, a stylist, struggle to know what to buy for myself? After all, I could shop and pick out items for other people all day long, every day. But when it came to me, I was a big blank, like a blue screen. Something waiting for someone else to create it. If I analyze the situation now, I recognize it was from a lack of self-confidence in my body and my judgment.

Yet more was at play, the thing that was shaking my core: a lack of knowing who the hell I was. However, let's table that for the time being and get down to the system that helped me purge my closet and start over.

The Purge

The first step to a fresh closet is getting rid of all the stuff that isn't you anymore, including the stuff that never was you in the first place. This purge can be painful, bringing memories and tough choices—"I wore that dress to my fortieth birthday party," or "That pair of shoes was so expensive"—but you'll feel much lighter on the other end of the process. Here are my tips for pushing through the purge.

Grab a friend.
For those of you who don't have a fashion stylist as a best friend, grab your most trusted and stylish friend (someone who will be honest about what looks good and what doesn't), woo him or her with promises of a cocktail and some laughs, and get down to it.

Get organized.
Make three sections or piles:
(1) Things you definitely like
(2) Things you don't wear or are questioning
(3) Things you look at and think, *Why is this still even here?*

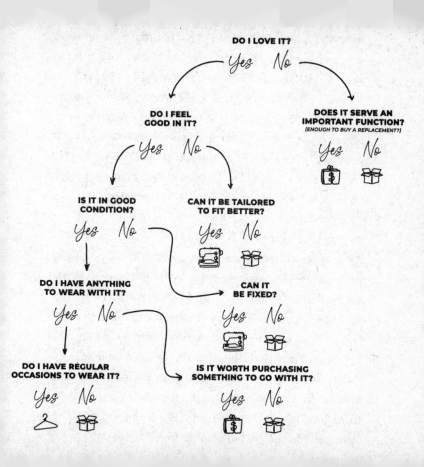

Try it on.

Ideally, try on everything in piles (2) and (3) that has a question mark. When it's on your body and you look in the mirror, if it makes you uncomfortable, makes you cringe, or you can't put your finger on why it's not you, *get rid of it*. Even if it still has the tags on it. Even if your mother gave it to you. Even if it was expensive. It's hard, but you can do it. And don't stop until you've tried on every sweater, blouse, skirt, pair of pants, and shoes in pile (2) and have double-checked that the other things belong in piles (1) and (3). The wonderful feeling you experience after you've purged will make each painful goodbye worth it.

Avoid the fantasy pitfall.

A common wardrobe mistake many of us make is to keep certain pieces for a fantasy life we might have at some point. For the fancy party we might get invited to, the camping trip we will go on someday, the luxe beach vacation we'll go on when we have the money. Or the big one for most of us: the clothes that will fit again once we lose that ten or twenty pounds we've been working on. Think hard about why you're holding on to certain pieces. Try to think like this: If you were helping a friend through the purge, would you encourage that friend to keep the piece or donate it?

Embrace where you are in life.

You used to have a desk job, but now you work from home and you're in your workout clothes all day. You don't need to keep those gray suits you wore six years ago "just in case" you return to the office. Even if you do return, those suits will be dated. You hang on to the leather pants or leather mini because you plan to get back on the treadmill four times a week . . . as soon as you have more time. Check in with yourself: Even if you do lose those ten pounds, is leather still your thing and do you have an occasion to wear it?

Enjoy the lighter feeling of less-is-more.

I don't have to explain the symbolism of discarding things from the married or previous you. But maybe even more powerful is the way that paring down creates this reverse-psychology-alternate-wardrobe-universe, where you feel as though you have more to wear, not less, because you like everything in your wardrobe.

Is it falling apart?

We all have items we love and feel good in. Sometimes we love them a little too much, and through the veil of our love, we can't see their flaws. We tend to wear our favorites into the ground. Really examine the item: Does it have moth holes? Does it smell musty? Do your favorite shoes have scuffs? Are they essentially falling apart? No matter how much you adore this piece or that pair of shoes, if the answer is yes to any of these questions, it has to go. The good news is you'll feel less guilty about buying a new, updated version of your favorite item.

Spot the holes.

While you're going through this process, have your friend help you spot the holes in your wardrobe and keep a list. For example, maybe you have lots of pretty blouses, but none of your current jeans or pants look good with any of them. Put the specific item "jeans to go with blouses" on your list. Or you have lots of skirts for work, but only one of your tops looks good with any of them, and after you wear that one top with a skirt, you're stuck wearing pants the rest of the week, and your other skirts go unworn. Then you'd add "more tops to go with work skirts" to the list. Some of the gaps in your wardrobe will be updated versions of pieces you already have. Be as specific as you can, so the shopping part is as easy as possible. Let your friend help you with this.

Your list might look something like this:

1. A versatile black leather ankle boot that you can wear with jeans, pants, skirts, and dresses—basically, with everything

2. Neutral suede or leather shoes that can be worn with that floral dress you love but never wear

The Edelman

need

3. Cool sneakers that will go with jeans or shorts for weekends running around to the farmers market or on errands

Camo chucks (handwritten)

4. A new pair of jeans, because your stylish friend told you all of your Old Navy ones are stretched out from so much wear

need (handwritten)

5. An updated spring jacket, because the only thing you have for spring is an old trench coat with a mustard stain on it, or a fleece that should be worn only when hiking or gardening, or a threadbare (not in a good way) jean jacket

need (handwritten)

6. And, most definitely, new undergarments, because the waistbands on your underpants are crunchy and your bras are all missing a clasp

✓ (handwritten)

Maintain and refresh as needed.

One of my clients compared the purging process to having a personal trainer come over to whip you into shape. At first you feel amazing. And for a while, you feel motivated to keep it up. Remember that you might need to purge again at some point, to reinvigorate yourself and get back on track. Once you've completed a purge, continual revamping and refreshing of your wardrobe doesn't have to be as involved. Maybe it's purchasing the one pair of chunky heels you need that will allow you to wear those three pairs of long pants so they don't drag on the ground.

Or it's an updated, great-fitting pair of jeans that makes all your tops feel new again. Or you realize you have accumulated twenty-three versions of the same black top and you need some color in your life. It will always feel indescribably cathartic to go through your closet and get rid of clothes that no longer fit the new you and identify the keepers that do. As you evolve and change, so will your closet.

Let the process open you up to rediscovery.

Along with the theme of "I don't even know who I am anymore," many questions that had nothing to do with clothes arose as I went through my closet, one pair of shoes, one pair of pants at a time, deciding what to keep and what to purge. What did I even like or want? Suddenly I had choices, but I didn't know the answers. What music *I* wanted to listen to, what *I* wanted to do on a Saturday with my kids, how *I* wanted to decorate my new apartment. Did *I* like eating meat almost every night for dinner? Did *I* want to listen to electronic dance music during dinner? Did *I* want to build a fort in the living room for the millionth time on Saturday morning and then be the one to clean it up?

Maybe I did want to do all of those things. But I needed to dive deep to find out.

You could panic and fall on the bed sobbing, because this whole "discovering yourself" process is exhausting.

And you'd be justified. And you can resent all of your still-married friends because, somehow, they managed to hang on to themselves throughout long relationships and becoming mothers. Or they simply "chose well." And you'd be justified again. But you also can approach your new circumstances as an expedition to discovering a whole new person. The one who was there all along, but asleep.

Ask Alyssa

Q: I'm embarrassed to tell people I'm online dating. Especially my married friends. How do I get over that, so I feel comfortable talking about it with my friends?

A: First of all, millions of people date online. When online dating first became a thing, it may have had a different reputation that some people haven't forgotten, but these days it is the way single people meet, and it no longer carries a negative connotation. Second of all, your friends should be thrilled that you are up for dating. They'd rather have you actively dating than have you curled up in the fetal position, depressed at home, right? Pick one friend you think will be the most encouraging and practice breaking the news about your online dating, before approaching your other friends. You might be surprised by how supportive they are.

Divorce Is the Mother of Reinvention

Like many other moms/wives, I'd spent my adult life building up my husband's career with him. Encouraging and supporting and doing the bulk of the childcare duties. There should be a college course: How to Not Ditch Your Own Career in Favor of Your Partner's. Still, I had made my bed, and I had to sleep in it. Only now, I needed a *new* bed, not to mention a mattress, pillows, and sheets, and I had to figure out how to pay for that bedding, along with everything else.

At that time, I could have blamed my lack of clients entirely on raising my kids, but that would have been a lie. The biggest reason was the previously mentioned lack of self-confidence—in my physical self, but mostly in my career self. I had constant self-doubt. Sometimes I'd convince myself I was a talentless impostor who didn't deserve to work in fashion, which was then reinforced when I didn't get new clients. Not a great cycle for trying to create a new life for myself after separating from my husband and going through the painful divorce process. I didn't have my own voice of encouragement, and my husband's voice of doubt still infiltrated my brain. I doubted myself as a mother, as a wife, as a person. I wasn't employable. And I was pretty sure I wasn't lovable.

Secret Smokes

For most people, the first step in looking for a job is updating a résumé or scrolling through job postings online. My first step was buying a pack of cigarettes. It was an old college habit that had reared its ugly head because of the stress of starting over. Smoking is gross, and I hated myself for doing it. It was the opposite of self-care. When my kids were with me, I'd arrive home and my daughter would tell me I smelled "like the subway." Thankfully, she didn't know that the smell of the subway was the smell of cigarette smoke. When my kids weren't with me, I'd get home at night, sit on my fire escape, and enjoy one last cigarette of the day, looking out over the backyards of my block.

Smoking was self-destructive, but, boy, did it feel good in the moment. I was miserable. I was looking for an apartment, dealing with finding out that my soon-to-be-ex-husband was already dating someone, listening to my oldest daughter cry herself to sleep at night about the separation. The stress of the divorce, the stress of my kids acclimating to their new life living in two homes, and the stress of looking for work was a lot to manage. I decided that if smoking during this time was helping me not be that heap on the floor, then so be it. I promised myself I'd stop as soon as I got through this beginning part of my new life.

I felt like I couldn't catch a break. I needed something good to happen.

A few days later, a fashion editor friend I'd known since my early days in New York City reached out to me. Magazines were folding left and right, but she'd pivoted into e-commerce and was now lead art director for a large retailer. She asked if I could put together a portfolio showcasing any fashion shoots I'd styled and art directed—*by the end of the week*. Yikes. And then come in to meet with her and her boss, the creative director. Double yikes. I'd always been terrible at interviews. I'd get nervous and hear myself and then get more down on myself and more nervous and blabber on until I was walking out and wondering what had just happened and imagining what the interviewer must think of me.

But now I *really* needed this opportunity to work out. In the state I was in, it would have to be a "fake it till you make it" scenario, the likes of which I'd never attempted. I had to fake confidence. I had to fake self-assuredness. And fake them well.

I walked into the slick downtown studio, palms sweating and my stomach in a knot. With her smiling face and relaxed vibe, my friend instantly put me at ease. It also helped that all the changes happening overwhelmed me so much that I didn't have the time or energy to obsess and overanalyze everything.

After we talked for a bit, she introduced me to her boss, a chic Frenchwoman who intimidated me right from the start. Still, I managed to keep it together, answering her questions with as much fake confidence as I could. At the end of the interview, I was invited to come in for a trial day. I could hardly believe it as I walked to the subway to head home. I'd pulled it off. They liked me and liked my work. They felt I was an accomplished stylist and art director and wanted me to work with them. I only needed to believe it myself.

A few weeks later, I was in their photo studio. Now *this* was familiar territory for me. I may have been doubting my skills, my talent, my ability, and my taste, but I felt at ease in a photo studio. For the first time, I spent the day not thinking about my divorce. I was around creative people, fun people. I almost felt like I was living a normal life. Toward the end of the day, my friend pulled me aside and said they'd love to hire me as a permalancer (long-term freelancer). I left the photo studio and walked to the subway as an art director. I was feeling damn good about myself.

Looking back, it's sort of a miracle this opportunity landed in my lap. And it's equally miraculous that I didn't screw it up. For those of you who don't self-sabotage, count your blessings. For those of you familiar with it, you know what it's like to "accidentally" arrive late to an interview or turn down a fantastic opportunity because you subconsciously feel you aren't good enough. I have done both and worse to undermine my own success. The old me would have thought I didn't deserve this lucky break. I would have found some way to sabotage the whole thing.

If you want to hear the most ridiculous story of self-sabotage ever, I'll tell you how, when I was twenty-seven, I turned down a full-time job as Christy Turlington's personal assistant. What's that? Why would a young woman trying to make it in the fashion world turn down a job with one of the biggest fashion icons in the world? You guessed it: I didn't feel I deserved it, and I sabotaged the opportunity. Instead, I said, "Thank you so much for the offer, but I'm trying to become a successful fashion stylist here." Yes, it's true. I've lost sleep over this one.

At the very least, if I'd still been living with my husband when this new permalancer opportunity came through, I would've gone home and heard words that would have made me question myself again. The seeds of doubt would have grown, and by the next time I went to the photo studio, I would have been bumbling around.

But I was on my own now and needed to feed my kids and pay my bills (and divorce lawyers aren't cheap). I went home to my new apartment and didn't hear a word about how I couldn't handle a job like that or that I shouldn't be leaving my kids three or four or five days a week. It felt so liberating to believe in myself.

Be Kind to Yourself on Your Road to Rediscovery

Forgive your coping mechanisms.

Give yourself permission not to feel guilty about turning to old habits or indulging yourself a bit if it helps you get through the first ugly, scary, stressful stages of rediscovering yourself. Whether it's a cigarette here and there, binge-watching Netflix, an extra glass of wine, standing in the shower until you've used all the hot water, or eating an entire bag of Oreos, forgive yourself for whatever less-than-perfect behaviors give you a little release and comfort. Of course, if your coping mechanisms veer into situations that are dangerous or addictive, turn to a friend to help you find a less destructive guilty pleasure. I'm thankful I was able to stop smoking almost immediately after signing the final divorce papers. Go figure.

Fake it till you make it.

If I hadn't believed I could fake self-confidence, I never would have been able to get through that all-important job interview. If I'd told myself I was good enough rather than *I can fake being good enough*, I never could have gone through with it. What's funny is that even though I had to fake my belief in myself, I *was* good enough, and my friend and her boss saw that. It wasn't long before I saw it for myself.

Turn to friends for help and support.

There can be a tendency to feel as though you have to get through this all by yourself. If you're going through a divorce, you'd better get used to doing things on your own, right? But if it hadn't been for my friend's kind offer to give me that interview and for her smiling face encouraging me, I don't know what would have happened. Accept the kindness and help of friends without feeling guilty or burdensome. You'd do the same for them, wouldn't you?

Be open to those windows of opportunity.

It's not always easy to see opportunities when you're curled up on the floor of your closet, staring at the white cowboy boots you've never worn. Try to keep an eye out for experiences and slivers of hope from unexpected places. Be open rather than dismissive when good things present themselves. Whether they're the universe throwing you a bone or plain dumb luck, seize on them and see where they lead.

Avoid self-sabotage.

This one is hard for those of us who've struggled with self-confidence or who've had other people make us doubt ourselves. Be conscious of old tendencies and concentrate on pushing them away.

Celebrate successes, even small ones.

Some days, washing my hair, shaving my legs, and putting on shoes felt like a victory. Praise and reward yourself when you accomplish something hard—finishing your closet purge, taking a brisk walk or a run, or going to a job interview. Let yourself have fun when something good happens.

Resist old negative voices.

Let go of those people and voices who make you feel bad. For me, it took a while before I could get my ex-husband's doubting judgments and undercutting out of my head. When I finally banished his voice from my mind (it didn't happen overnight), I could replace it with my own voice and the positive feedback from supportive people in my life. Positive self-talk can help drown out the old, negative voices.

Get in your comfort zone.

We all have that place or activity where we feel our best, where we feel at home and in our element. For me, it was the photo shoot. Even though I doubted my abilities at first, I was in my happy place. That meant I could forget all the stressful stuff going on and focus instead on what I loved doing. It doesn't have to be a job. It can also be enjoying a hobby, playing a sport, running, being in nature, painting, crafting—whatever and wherever it is that you feel in the zone. It could be something you used to do that you'd like to pick up again.

Start a new exercise routine.

You might be groaning at me right now, and I don't blame you. But hear me out. I never loved working out. I'd do it reluctantly, only as a means to an end. But while I was going through my divorce, I started exercising in a whole new way. I did it for the physical changes—I got stronger every week. Most of all, though, I did it for the emotional help it gave me. The stronger I felt physically, the stronger I felt mentally. I found that while I was working out, I'd think, *If I can keep going with this set or the next mile or the next thirty seconds, I can do anything.* Even take on my ex-husband in front of a judge and a room full of lawyers. I now understand why so many people exercise all the time. It really is empowering and can keep your sanity intact. A brisk walk is a great way to start a new exercise routine and work the body and the mind.

Art Appreciation

In my fantasy postdivorce world, I would be living the Meg Ryan single–New Yorker role in *When Harry Met Sally*. Even though the character she plays isn't a divorced mom, for me she represents what a single woman in a metropolitan city can be. She is independent but vulnerable. She has style and smarts. Like her, I was going to wander through museums by myself on the weekends I didn't have my kids. I was going to be sophisticated and worldly, but also fun and carefree. That's not asking for much, is it? I would be in a cream, over-sized, cashmere turtleneck, brown suede boots, and a knit beanie, crunching through fall leaves on my way from the subway to The Met.

What I didn't realize is that on those weekends I'd be so sad and lonely without my daughters that the thought of doing anything alone was unbearable. I had to make plans with a friend (or go on a date) every day that my kids were away from me. At least for the first year. However, I did remain hopeful that I would still stroll through galleries solo "someday."

Art had been a big part of my life throughout my twenties. After an art theory professor inspired me, I signed up for a collaging class and soon after a welding class and made some crazy metal sculptures. Once I moved to New York and no longer had time or money for these classes, I took my collage skills and started making homemade cards in the evenings. It was something, pre-kids, that gave me a lot of comfort and a chance to express myself on paper. I thought that, when I had kids, we'd sit together and make cards. We did a couple of times early on. But when you're miserable in your marriage, it's an energy killer. I had little motivation to get up in the morning, never mind drag out all of my bins of pretty papers and collage materials.

After a few months of being single, it dawned on me that one way I could experience art again was through my two daughters and their creativity. I started being more present when I was with them. I'd focus on them and what they wanted to create. I'd sit and mold clay, paint with watercolors, and make tiny furniture out of toothpicks, corks, and cardboard. All things I'd done occasionally when I was married, but in a distracted way. Now I was all in. I rekindled my love for making art and craft projects. To this day, the three of us will sit and paint together by watching step-by-step YouTube videos. Rediscovering my love of art in a totally different way, with them as part of the experience, was incredibly healing for me and my girls.

When *Journaling* Became My Verb of the Moment

You know your fantasy version of life, where each night, you sit at your bedside and thoughtfully write down your hopes and dreams? A candle gently flickers nearby and perhaps a perfectly askew cashmere throw covers your feet? Yeah, that was never me either.

At various points in my life, I'd tried to journal, but my words always sounded unnatural, like a "Dear Diary" moment. However, this being my new life, I decided to give it another go. One day, I grabbed one of my daughters' half-used school composition books and began to write. Even though, or maybe because, I wasn't someone who'd kept a journal my whole life, I felt empowered by it. I soon found that journaling wasn't merely a way to vent horrible thoughts about my ex and daydream about meeting my possible soul mate but also an adjunct to therapy.

I went out and bought a real journal. Mine was a pretty pale blue with gold-leaf pages and gold lettering on the front. But use whatever works for you. Here are some topics I found helpful to think about and journal on that ended up being very healing:

- **Think and write about what you want from yourself.** Here is a fresh start for you to think about how you want to be and present yourself in the world. Are there career goals you've wanted to achieve? Maybe you'd like to develop more self-confidence? Worry less?
- **Think and write about what you're looking for in a partner.** Such as "a person who makes me

laugh," "someone who will support me in my dreams," or "someone who likes to travel."

- **Think and write about what you want from dating.** Sex? A companion? A life partner?
- **Think and write about what you want in general.** Whether it's a material concern like a new sofa; a dream activity, such as traveling more; going back to school; or something more abstract, there's no limit to how much you can write, how much you can want for your life.
- **Write down what you want to feel in your new life.** Perhaps you want to feel more sexy after not feeling that for so long. Or you want to feel more adventurous. Whatever it is, writing it down is the first step in making it a reality.
- **Describe how you want to look in your new life.** A new haircut or color? Some new makeup tricks? Or maybe it's simply looking "happy" again. In the first six months after I left my husband, several people told me they thought I'd had cosmetic work done on my face. No, it was just me being happy, and it showed on my face.
- **List new actions and goals you want to have in your new life.** The obvious are career goals or a new exercise regimen. But they could also be more general: "Take more time to read on the

weekends," "Eat more vegetarian meals," or "Set aside time to meditate."

- **Write without censoring yourself.** Your new journal will accept you for who you are and won't judge you. That may sound silly, I know, but it's important to remember.

The process should give you comfort, not anxiety, so start simple. Write one sentence a day. Or even one word. I began by writing thoughts out in list form, to ease the pressure of the Dear Diary moment. Try free writing, where you write without concern for perfect punctuation or correct grammar. No one else will be reading this. I give you permission to make mistakes and cross out words or sentences. Overthinking your journaling makes it unenjoyable. Make it as lighthearted as you can.

Once you start your online dating journey, keep journaling through it—the good dates and the bad, the funny texts and the repulsive photos. It's also helpful to look back on past entries to see if you're staying on track or if you want to make adjustments. Maybe you realized your list of wants in a partner has shifted since you began meeting actual human beings for dates. It's also gratifying to see how far you've come, day by day or month by month. It's incremental, and sometimes it keeps you motivated to see the progress.

If I haven't yet convinced you to keep a journal, consider this: ten years from now, think how entertaining it will be to read through your thoughts and experiences from this crazy but exciting, and occasionally horrific, transition in your life. At the least, having a record of this time in your life will prove to you that you overcame some really dark shit. When I read back through some of my journals from a few years ago, I'm reminded of how strong I was to get back out there and with such force. And how hilarious—or plain fun—some of those moments were.

Redecorate

After looking for an apartment for the whole month of December in snowy, cold weather—and I'm thankful that my best friend stopped me from rushing into the first crappy apartment I saw—I found a sunny, cozy, top-floor brownstone apartment in Brooklyn, with an extremely decrepit closet I came to love.

Many people might feel sad moving from a beautiful house to an apartment that was a quarter the size in a decaying brownstone with crumbling front steps that seemed like a lawsuit waiting to happen. Yet I couldn't have been happier. To me, the apartment was perfect. I was terrified of making this major move, but I was also excited at all the possibilities. One being how I'd take exactly half of my married-life belongings and make it into a home I'd love being in with my daughters *and* enjoy being in alone. A whole new concept.

At the advice of friends, who were worried I'd fall back into my usual "I can't spend money on myself" tendency, I allowed myself two splurges for the new place. I picked out paint colors to cheer up the white walls and had someone come measure for custom window shades—upgrades I *never* would have made without others' encouragement but that satisfied me when I walked into my home each evening. Having pretty paint colors and perfectly fit window shades made the flaws of the old apartment fade away. I also bought a few IKEA light fixtures to replace the awful, round boob-like ceiling fixtures.

Postdivorce is a smart time to be thrifty, but it doesn't have to equal sad and depressing. Think of online and brick-and-mortar secondhand stores, Etsy, and IKEA shopping as a way of saving for your future life. Get creative, obsess over Pinterest boards, and watch home improvement YouTube clips. I took my old furniture and made it feel new again. I put a new lampshade on an old lamp, a friend gave me a beautiful throw pillow for my bed, and I made a makeshift slipcover for the chair in my bedroom, with a tapestry I had stashed away, just to name a few of the minor decorative tweaks that made all the difference. For the shades in my bedroom, I ordered the blackout kind so I could sleep in on the weekends I didn't have my kids. (*Ahh.* Sleeping in. Unheard of in my married life.)

While moving out of my "marital home," as they call it in the lawyer's office, I was conscious of keeping my own books that I had read before having children or started to read and never finished once I had my children. When I settled into my apartment, I color coordinated my books into stacks on my one bookcase. I have always loved that arrangement. It was another one of those details that seems so small, but every time I looked over at those stacks, seeing them made me feel organized and reassured. Rearranging what you currently have, repainting something old, or fixing something broken or wobbly are all great, inexpensive ways to bring new life into your home. And one or two well-considered splurges like blackout shades? So worth it.

Take Up a New Hobby

Let me start by saying that I hate when people giving postdivorce advice tell you to "take up a new hobby." But, in the spirit of starting anew, I embraced this advice and decided on . . . guitar lessons. I had always wanted to play the guitar. Even just one song—one Neil Young song.

I imagined myself the next time I was upstate at a friend's house, sitting by the fire at night, whipping out

my guitar. I'd be like Joni Mitchell, wearing denim over-
alls and my hair in braids. I'd be lulling my friends and our
children with the perfect folk song. I found a flyer at my
local natural food store and contacted the teacher. I
bought a used guitar off of Craigslist and was ready for my
first lesson.

The truth is, I suck at guitar. And I eventually stopped
getting lessons because a) I really couldn't afford it, b) I
would never be a virtuoso, and c) a few months in, I saw
the teacher on one of the dating apps I was on, and it suddenly felt very awkward. But I had the guitar, so at night,
after my daughters were asleep, it was my way of calming
myself before bed. With my tea and a candle burning and
the lights dim, I'd practice my chords. It reminded me of
the days when I was nursing my daughter alone in the
dark living room at night and how meditative that was
for me (okay, sometimes, if I wasn't falling asleep). No
iPhone. No distractions. Simply a warm and cozy respite
from the chaos of my divorce.

It wasn't only about the clothes or the guitar or the bohemian apartment. The guitar and the apartment both
symbolized who I wanted to be in my new life. The girl
with the flowy hair and embroidered guitar strap, who was
a little wild and open to new things, but at the same time,
the freshly single mom scraping it together to make a cozy,
safe life for my kids, coming home after work, walking up
four flights of stairs to my attic-like apartment, climbing

out on the fire escape to smoke a cigarette before making my tea and practice my new folk song. That was the new persona I wanted to embody. I know I sound like a broken Neil Young record, but leaving a marriage is the perfect time to try many different personas.

Experiment and Reconnect with Cooking (or Don't)

For the first time, I subscribed to a weekly meal service that gave me the recipe and the groceries, and walked me through all the prep and cooking steps. This was exactly what I needed to regain my confidence in the kitchen. Before living with my ex, I'd cooked a lot. Back then, in my early twenties, I used to try new dishes here and there and also cook my old standbys. But I had since lost all trust in my cooking abilities. If you've ever lived with a "home chef" type, you know what I'm talking about: he (or she) owns the kitchen and is the one who cooks in there. However, you're allowed to go in and clean up after the show ends.

Over the years, the times I did cook were met with such dismay that eventually I believed I was a horrible cook. With the meal kits, however, I was cooking real dishes that tasted good. After making a few decent meals, I tried some of my old-time winners: mushroom-Gruyère quiche, homemade hummus, and French toast. The positive reactions from my daughters and friends I had over for dinner emboldened me and motivated me to try even more complicated dishes.

I started paying attention to what friends served when I went to their homes. One summer Saturday, having arrived late the night before at my friend Elana's beach house after a long week at my new-ish job, I sat at her kitchen island, decompressing from the week. On the island lay a new issue of a cooking magazine, open to a recipe for corn with mint and ricotta salata. The accompanying photo was so vibrant I could almost taste the fresh corn—with just enough crunch.

As we chatted in her kitchen, Elana lightly boiled the corn and scraped the kernels off the cobs for the salad. While watching her, seemingly absentmindedly, I was taking everything in. I saw my daughter whiz by in a neon-pink two-piece with her water gun flailing behind her, Elana's son hot on her heels as Elana finished making the recipe. When I took a few bites of the simple salad she'd whipped up, I thought, *I could pull this off.* I didn't have a beach house, but I could make this salad that went with a beach house, that had the breezy, free feel of a beach house.

When I got home, I subscribed to *Bon Appétit* and was excited to plan out meals I'd contribute when I was invited to my friends' vacation homes that summer. Before, I had been sort of jealous of these beach-house friends, but now I felt lucky to have friends who invited me over. If I hadn't gotten divorced, maybe I would've had a weekend house outside the city someday, somewhere. But I'd chosen my personal growth and sanity rather than that life. And right now, I was especially grateful for that. A subscription to a cooking magazine was a small step, but it became symbolic of my independence. I was no chef because of it, but the meal planning and cooking for other people was another discovery that empowered me.

If, on the other hand, your old self was responsible for cooking all the family meals, maybe it would empower you to take a break from cooking. Takeout, especially if you previously considered that a luxury or a dereliction of your "duties," can be a pleasant treat. You may never want to cook again! Or maybe you've been making meat and potatoes for your family for fifteen years, and now you want to try more vegetarian dishes or ethnic cuisine or new challenges like pasta-making or sourdough bread. Cook and eat what *you* want for a change.

Try New Things and See What Fits

Always wanted to go to a club, dancing until the wee hours of the morning? Host a casual dinner party for friends? Run a half marathon? Visit a touristy spot in your own town? Longed to get a second piercing? None of the above?

Try on a new persona like a new dress. See what fits. One of my clients, Julia, had lived in a huge house in Westchester with her CEO husband for twenty-five years. She'd been a stay-at-home mom, who hosted Martha Stewart–style dinners for up to twenty people for her husband's clients. She'd kept up a certain Park Avenue appearance that was expected of her, and her closet's contents reflected that. When Julia found out her husband was having a long-term affair, and with her kids away at college, she left him and moved to a loft downtown in the city. She started a retail job at a Soho boutique. She went out dancing with her friends at night. She said she'd never again host a dinner party.

However, trying new things doesn't have to be that dramatic. For instance, if you're craving new surroundings, a change could be as simple as finding a new home decorator who inspires you and following him or her on social media. It could motivate you to try painting one wall in your home or even daydream about what you could do.

Sometimes it's not something new that reinvigorates you: it's something old you bring back again. On my first Christmas as a single mom with my kids, we had opened our gifts and were lying around eating Christmas cookies and watching bad Christmas movies when my friend Jocelyn texted to see if we wanted to come for drinks and dessert with her and her family. My kids and I bundled up and walked the ten minutes to her house. Upon our arrival, her husband handed me one of his amazing cocktails.

A few hours later, Jocelyn and I—who were, just maybe, possibly, a little tipsy at this point—were in her bathroom, and she was holding a needle to my ear telling me she thought I should repierce my ears. I hadn't worn earrings in fifteen years because my ex told me they looked weird on me and I believed him. Jocelyn was convinced it was a great idea. I winced and gritted my teeth, waiting for the needle to hurt. My oldest daughter watched us, laughing and a bit nervous. It might have been the alcohol numbing the pain, but the needle went through painlessly. We took it as a sign that I had to start wearing earrings again. And wear earrings I did. All the time, and still do. In fact, it's something my new partner loves on me.

Another new thing I tried on was a pair of shoes. But not the kind of shoes you'd likely think a newly single New York City stylist would be buying.

I was never a person who enjoyed running. I ran track in high school for one season, because I didn't feel athletic enough to try out for soccer (cue the low self-esteem music again). I wasn't cut out for track overall, but the one thing I was decent at was sprinting. Long distance has never been for me, but I loved the rush that came from running as fast as I could.

Now, twenty-five years later, I started doing it again. Running made me sort of miserable yet was so satisfying when I finished. During my divorce, it gave me the strength and forward motion I needed after being a heap on the floor, not only in that moment in my new closet but essentially for eighteen years during my relationship with my ex. Running made me feel like I was moving in the right direction.

A few weeks into trying this new thing, I found myself asking one of my runner friends to help me pick out the perfect running shoe. Two things I wouldn't have done when I was married: buy something I didn't "need" and get out of my own way to try something new.

Date Old Boyfriends (Said No One Ever)

I didn't set out to do it. It just sort of happened.

When my husband and I made the difficult decision to separate, he started dating immediately. By *immediately*, I mean before we even moved out of the house and into separate apartments. How did he already feel like dating?!

A mere six weeks later, right after I moved into my own place, something clicked. Choosing the paint colors on my own—a girly lavender gray for the living room and a beautiful minty green for my daughters' room—was nothing short of thrilling. Deciding to put the rug this way and the reading lamp over there was like Christmas morning for me. No one telling me where to hang the pictures felt liberating. Typically in bed by 9:00 p.m. every night while I was married, I was finding myself wide awake, reading self-help books or decorating my living room or watching a new Netflix series until 1:00 a.m. My life suddenly invigorated me.

Each morning I woke up in my own bed, knowing the day ahead belonged to me. I was energized and empowered by the realization of my new freedom and the opportunity to reclaim my life, even redefine it. And it wasn't only my mind and spirit reawakening. My body felt electrified. I was twenty-five again. After years of not feeling in any way sexual, I was obsessed. All I could think about was dating and men and sex. I couldn't believe how this person inside me had lain dormant for so many years. But now she was back. And she was wearing motorcycle boots.

As I began to wonder what else about myself had been hiding beneath my identity as wife and mother, I let myself daydream about how I'd meet all the men I'd been missing out on over the years. Two words never entered those daydreams: *online dating*.

The last time I'd been on the dating scene, cell phones were a novelty, and swiping wasn't a thing. I was going to do it the old-fashioned way: one of my friends would have a single friend at work, and we'd be set up. I'd be swimming in blind dates.

Or so I thought.

My new closet beautifully purged, I moved on to the other rooms. One afternoon, I was unpacking boxes, ruthlessly discarding whatever wasn't going to fit into my new life, when I got an unexpected text. It was from an old boyfriend—let's call him Tall, Dark & Exceptionally Handsome (TD&EH). I hadn't talked to him in years. I'd heard that he'd separated from his wife. "Happy New Year!" the text said. "Hope you're well. Would love to grab a drink sometime." I immediately called our one mutual friend, thinking she'd spilled the beans. No, she hadn't told him my husband and I had broken up. I was floored. He'd reached out to me days after I'd moved out on my own? It felt like fairy-tale magic, like fate. I replied right away that I'd love to grab a drink.

Dating was going to be just like riding a bike.

The texts with TD&EH in the lead-up to our date became a little flirty—my first time ever doing this with someone. Every day I was having cheesy daydreams at work, about how, when I saw TD&EH, we'd lock eyes and he'd say something like, "Check, please," without looking away and then whisk me off to his loft downtown. I blabbed to all my work friends that I was meeting up with an old boyfriend, and one of the hair and makeup artists offered to do me up after work before the date. I may have been a *little* excited.

Our date was at Indochine, a sceney New York restaurant popular with models and celebrities. It's the kind of place where you'd see either someone who's famous or someone who should be/could be famous. It was also a place I hadn't been to since before I'd become a married mom. The walls were papered with leafy green Miami-style palm fronds. Nowadays, it would be an Instagrammer's dream. But this place was old school. They don't allow that kind of thing in there.

I texted TD&EH when I was in the taxi on my way to meet him. My new self was intrigued. And also a little confused—he'd mentioned his friend from out of town would be there, with his "mistress." It seemed strange how nonchalant he was calling his friend's companion that, but I buried the icky feeling. After all, I was soon on the arm of my very tall ex-boyfriend, who was as jaw-droppingly handsome as he'd been nearly twenty years before, only now with gray hair. So what if he didn't bother to hide that he was checking out our lanky waitress with the sexy Afro at Indochine? TD&EH was a man who loved women. He couldn't help himself, and I conveniently chose to ignore it.

When we sat down, he was surprised and happy to hear I'd separated from my husband. He exchanged glances with his friend across the table. It was my first real-life flirtation in ages. I felt so alive I didn't bother wondering why he'd asked me on a date, if he'd thought I was still married.

After TD&EH's friend and the "mistress" left, he told me how unhappy he and his wife were.

"Wife? I thought you were separated." I'd already let my mind become consumed with thoughts of going home with him. For the past week.

TD&EH explained that they'd gotten back together after separating. He wanted an open marriage, but she didn't. They fought about it endlessly. That was the first time the red siren appeared, wailing in my head: *Run for your life!* I felt like one of those cartoon characters who's running full speed and then looks down and the ground had ended steps before—and he's staring at the cavern below that he's about to fall into.

I couldn't hide my disappointment that he was married—or that his being married wasn't stopping him from seeing other women. As thrilling as the magnetism had been, I was beginning to see that being a sex-crazed single mom wasn't all freedom and sexy bars. I knew then that jumping back into the dating scene was going to be more complicated than my daydreams had led me to believe. I needed to figure out what I wanted in "real life," not only in my dreams.

What I Want: Write Down
What You're (Actually) Looking For

I found journaling about what I wanted out of dating to be extremely helpful for making my dating daydreams stay on track with what I wanted in real life. At this point in your dating life, are you looking for someone to talk to? Someone to run with or go to the movies with or cook with? Your soul mate? Someone to have sex with? Be honest with yourself and enjoy the freedom of putting your real thoughts on paper without harsh judgment. And yes—leave out the part about old boyfriends.

What you're looking for may shift in the process. At first, I really, really just wanted to have sex with someone and leave that "first time" behind me. Later, I wanted to find someone to have dinner with and maybe invite to a night out with my friends. Finally, that became finding my "Can you hang with my kids, my sometimes crazy, creative friends, and my new-agey mother, and still be fun, smart, and sexy?" soul mate.

When you're writing your list of things you want, remember that you're not ordering a burrito. You can't be as picky and precise. There will be concessions made, unlike specifying a type of cheese and beans. On the other hand, of course, "sense of humor" can mean different things to different people. As can "good-looking" and "kind." To me, "kind" meant someone who genuinely valued my thoughts and opinions. To others, "kind" might mean volunteering at a local soup kitchen.

Later, feel free to tear this page out of your journal and burn it. But for the moment, use it as a guide while on your dating journey.

Every time you meet someone, or when you're swiping or chatting with the cashier at your local bodega, observe that person as if you're a zoologist observing animals in the wild. Note the qualities in people who stand out and how certain people make you feel. It became fun to me to meet all these different types of people and learn about myself in the process. And don't set your expectations too high. The most perfect man in the world is going to disappoint you in some way. Even a Ken doll, the poured polymer version of a perfect man, has flaws (in his case, having no genitalia).

It can also be helpful to write a list of the things you *don't* want in a partner. Sometimes we're so caught up in our list of wants that we overlook the qualities we decidedly don't want in someone. For example, I wanted someone who was motivated and career oriented. I guess *successful* would be the word to use. However, I failed to mention that I didn't want someone who was obsessed with work or a workaholic. Oops. Our "don't wants" can be as important as our "wants."

Ask Alyssa

Q: I know you say that not many single people meet someone in real life anymore. But I still really hope that will happen for me, so I've been putting off online dating for years. What do you think I should do?

A: There's no reason you can't keep putting out into the world that you will meet your next partner at the grocery store. But while you're doing that, you can also have a dating profile up. Especially when most of these sites are free.

My friends did set me up with people a couple of times, but other than that, the only time in two and a half years of dating that I met someone in real life was when my daughters' former babysitter Veronica was visiting us from Sweden. I took her out to a cool, new restaurant with a DJ and a bit of a scene. I thought it would be fun for a twenty-two-year-old (and apparently a forty-two-year-old divorcee?). Veronica and I were eating at the bar when some guys a few stools down sent over tequila shots. For the record, I do not do shots, and neither does Veronica. But this night, we seized our New York moment and went for it. We danced the night away with our new friends and gave them our phone numbers as we said goodbye. Veronica had to ask the taxi driver to stop only once on our way home, for

her to puke out the door. We could have been in an episode of *Girlfriends' Guide to Divorce*. Maybe not one of my
finer postdivorce moments, but it sure was fun. And I did
hear from the guy the next day. So, do people meet in real
life? I'd say about once every two and a half years, and it
may require tequila shots and dancing with your Swedish
babysitter.

Newly Single in a New World

Even though I'd built my career in fashion, art direction,
and styling for magazines, advertising, and celebrity clients, I was at square one when it came to styling my own
new life. As a single woman for the first time in almost
twenty years, the world of selfies, bios, and dating apps
was foreign and daunting. There was a steep learning
curve and a lot of trial and error, but once I got the hang of
things and could use my years of experience to help myself, I discovered I could help others too.

In the beginning, however, I was right where most of
my clients are when they first come to see me: staring into
the scary abyss of my new single life and, even scarier, online dating. I had to think of myself as the client.

The idea of online dating loomed large. I wanted to get back out into the world, but online dating made me feel like a freshman going to a school dance for the first time. I didn't know where to start, how it worked, what would happen, or what to wear. It would take an experienced single friend, all my professional experience as a stylist, and some serious rediscovery of who I now was to create a profile and start swiping.

My online dating journey officially began after some rough starts in the "old-fashioned" dating world (TD&EH, for example). One day, while sitting on barstools at a no-frills Brooklyn bar, the kind that is dark even on a sunny day and always has a few locals sitting at the end of the bar, I was telling my Cool Single Friend (CSF), with whom I'd reconnected after my divorce, about my desire to jump-start my new dating life. I told her how I couldn't even find a one-night stand. What was wrong with me?

I knew she'd have some answers. CSF was perpetually dating someone and made being single look so freaking fun. She grabbed my phone and set up a Tinder profile for me, right there in the bar. I guess I knew all along I'd have to do it at some point, but I didn't think it would be a few months after becoming single. And I certainly didn't think of starting with Tinder. But at that point, I was still consumed with dating and men and sex, so I had to take charge. Might as well go for the gusto with Tinder. And she made it seem so easy.

"Don't worry about the bio," CSF said, scrolling through pics of me on my phone to find one for the profile. "If you're a woman looking for a guy, you don't even need a bio. They only look at your picture." Well, that sounded depressing, but my friend was a seasoned swiper in this age of apps, so I went with whatever she said. I watched in scared anticipation. In minutes, she'd posted my profile. Dying of curiosity, I sat next to her as we swiped through photos of men. It was beyond exciting to see the little bubbles with my face and my match's face pop up when we matched.

"Whatever you do," she said, "don't message first. The guy should always make the first move." I nodded, taking in everything she said.

Let's Do This

So, I was ready! No longer a heap on the floor, I had everything in place: Perfectly curated, single-woman closet, check. Cute and comfy boho-chic apartment, check. Boss in the kitchen, check. I was a stylist, now an art director, a home chef, a decorator, a runner. And every time I saw those bright orange running shoes by my front door, I felt proud. They had clocked some actual miles. That strong, single woman who'd gone out and bought them had taken them home and used them. A few times a week! Good for her!

Maybe I wasn't a restaurant-worthy chef, and mostly a chef for two small people. And maybe I wasn't going to be the next Martha Stewart of home decorating and entertaining. But I was a working single mom, and I was putting myself out there in the online dating world. No, wait. I wasn't merely going to start online dating—I was going to crush this online dating thing. If I could master a corn salad with mint and ricotta salata, having a string of great, sexy, flirty dates would be a breeze. The world was my oyster! Speaking of, I wanted to go out for oysters! I wanted to wear a cute dress out on a date to get oysters. Heck, yeah, I was winning. I was finally going to have unmarried (and hopefully hot) sex. I had painted walls, a closet full of too-dressy clothes, money coming in (albeit in very small amounts), and a Tinder profile.

My message to the men of the world: I'm hibernating no more.

Readers, let's do this.

Rediscover Your Style Cheat Sheet

- Face your closet and purge everything that's not you. — do

- Rediscover who you are—or reinvent yourself altogether—being kind to yourself in the process.

- Journal your way through, writing down your thoughts — get and emotions and also what you want for yourself and your life.

- Redecorate, even in minor ways, to create an — do atmosphere that reflects what makes you feel happy, cozy, and warm in your new life.

- Try new things: new hobbies, new ways of cooking — do or not cooking, new personas. Try them on and see what fits.

- Give yourself time to think deeply about who you are, — always who you want to be, and what you want from life, from a partner, from yourself. Rediscovering yourself, especially after ending a long-term relationship, can be a scary time, but it's also exciting and full of new possibilities.

2

Style Your Look

Finding the Freedom to Feel Good

Standing in front of yet another mirror, in a small, chic Tribeca boutique, I was turning around and looking at my butt in a pair of dark gray jeans. It looked good! I looked good. I *felt* good. My friend Jocelyn was outside the door, asking how it was going. I double-checked to make sure the mirror wasn't one of those deceptively flattering ones that department stores always seem to have. It wasn't. The good butt was real!

It was the first Saturday without my daughters since the split. And it was probably only the third weekend ever, since they were born, that I wasn't with them. I had been

preparing for an afternoon of self-pity. The last thing I'd
expected that day was to feel happy, let alone sexy. I'd wo-
ken up miserable and planned to stay that way all day. But
Jocelyn swooped in and insisted we go shopping. Numb
and not feeling like doing much of anything, I agreed—on
the condition we would go for wine after. But then this
surprise: those jeans. Those jeans were definitely me. Correction—these jeans were definitely the *new* me.

I told Jocelyn I was absolutely buying them. I'd be buying them with the paycheck from my new job. This may
not seem like a big deal, but for me, at that moment, I realized what independence felt like: exciting and empowering and sexy. I felt really freaking sexy. And it had been
a while since I could say that.

After helping me choose an apartment, pack and un-
pack boxes, purge my "married mom" closet, pierce my
ears, and then keep me from jumping off several cliffs,
Jocelyn was not only my lifeline but now had taken on the
strange job of being a stylist's stylist. As a New York City
stylist and fashion editor, I should have been shopping all
the time. Or at least part of the time. Some of the time?
However, as a mother of two with anxiety about money, I'd
gotten into the habit of depriving myself. I think a lot of
moms can relate to the guilt about spending money on
yourself rather than on your kids. Jocelyn was helping me
get over that.

The store where we shopped that day was among the places I took my clients, but I'd never shopped there for myself. Another self-worth thing. Over the years, I'd hardly ever treated myself, even when I could have. Now, as I envisioned my new life ahead, trying on clothes went from being *meh* at best and anxiety-inducing at worst, to being very exciting. I settled on that pair of dark gray jeans that fit just right. I felt like those jeans understood me in a way my husband never did. They got me. I needed things in my life that got me. And even though it was indulgent, I did it anyway. I deserved it.

It was January, so I also bought a couple of sexy sweaters. At the time, I wasn't thinking of these for dating per se; I was thinking of what I felt good in. But every time I went out on a first date, I wore those jeans and one of those sweaters. They were symbolic of my new life: I bought them guilt-free, I felt great in them, and they were exactly what I needed.

The freedom to feel good in your own clothes is one of the keys to looking good in them. I dated this one divorced guy, Nick, who wore black button-down shirts on all our dates. One weekend Nick and I had a daytime date, and instead of his black button-down he wore a T-shirt and jeans. He seemed so much more relaxed and himself in this daytime attire. After a couple of months of dating, I confessed to him that, as a stylist, I thought the black button-downs didn't suit him or his personality. Nick said his ex-wife had told him she liked only the black button-downs on him, and she'd bought him six that he rotated. He told me he'd never felt comfortable in them and that he was so relieved to have the freedom to change it up. He simply needed someone to say something. Nick now wears T-shirts all the time, even to work. Button-downs, specifically black ones, are a thing of his past.

One of my male clients, Chris, a professor in New York City, wore mostly black V-neck T-shirts in his off-hours. When we met to work on his profile, we photographed him in the T-shirt as well as in a button-down and then in a sweatshirt. When we finished taking photos and were scrolling through them together—before I even had a chance to say anything—he was shocked to see that the pictures of him in the black T-shirt were the least flattering. We realized that it made his neck look extra, extra long. When he left that day, his parting words were, "Well, if nothing else, I realized after fifteen years that I've been wearing the exact wrong thing for my body type."

Discovering what is out there and what you feel good in is the first step in styling your new self. Allowing yourself to invest in a new outfit is part of valuing yourself and the process of putting yourself out in the world. Most of my female clients, many of them moms like me, have a difficult time spending money on themselves. I've been there myself, as I've mentioned. But this is the time to treat yourself more than ever. Give yourself permission to buy at least one or two new pieces. Feeling good about yourself is a worthy investment. You're not going to be a better mother, wife, girlfriend, boss, or employee if you're feeling bad. You must make it a priority to treat yourself once in a while. You've earned that massage, hair color, new dress, or glass of wine with a friend. We all need a go-to outfit that we know fits us—inside and out. Those jeans and sexy sweater that we shine in every time.

Ask Alyssa

Q: Going through my divorce, I've put on a few pounds, stress eating and not making time to exercise. The idea of going shopping for a new wardrobe or outfit is so depressing. How can I make it more fun even though I know I've gone up a size or two?

A: This is something I've been hearing from clients for years, divorced or not. So many people come to me saying, "I really want to do this, but I'm going to wait until I lose this ten/twenty/thirty pounds." You're not alone.

Even though this could be a difficult time when you don't feel all that comfortable about yourself, it's also a time of freedom to get to know yourself again and to feel good about the qualities you'd forgotten you had. When you're trying on clothes, think about how far you've come, your new independence, or whatever it is about your new life that you're excited about. Think about how fun it is to create the new version of you. Remember to try on lots of different styles, colors, and brands. You never know what's been there for you, that perfect dress or perfect blouse, that you never thought to try before.

There is so much you will be missing out on if you wait until you've lost weight. Not to sound trite, but when it comes to looking fantastic, it's really, truly, honestly about how you feel inside that radiates out. I've discovered in my own experience that, sure, there are some people who only look for "model types" when online dating, but for most people, what attracts them on profile pics and on real-life dates are people's smiling faces and looking friendly and approachable, not model-thin bodies.

Keep Fashion Fantasies in Check

When I was newly single, going shopping for myself was actually a new way for me to feel sexy. Remember, I had lost *all* of my mojo being married. I hardly ever felt sexy.

Now that had all changed, and I was wearing clothes I had chosen because of how I felt in them. I was feeling better about myself than I had since college. It was a feeling I was really getting into.

In my fantasy single life, I was going to be invited to lots of cocktail parties. Of course, I would need cute skirts and dresses and heels to wear to these parties. On one of my trips with Jocelyn to Century 21, a designer discount store in New York City, I found a super sexy black pencil skirt with a black lace overlay and a pair of four-inch black strappy heels. To go with it, I bought a black-and-white boxy cropped top that hit the skirt right at the waist (a very flattering pairing). I also found a pair of metallic, strappy heels, a frilly, silk, button-down blouse, and a pleated, ivory leather skirt. I was going to be killing it at these cocktail parties. I would blow everyone away with my chic party looks.

Do you know how many cocktail parties I went to in those first years of being single? Exactly zero. It's okay. I'm not sad about it. I am sad that I spent money on those items that I think I wore once or twice each. So, that's why I'm giving you this advice: Try on things that make you feel sexy. Strut around the dressing room. Take some selfies. Maybe even buy one or two of them if it's in your budget. But remember to shop for the life you have, not the life you dream about when you sleep at night. We are all guilty of owning things in our closet that still have the tags on. I attribute this in part to the made-up lives we all wish or hope for.

Feel Badass in Your Clothes (and Out of Them)

Now for the feeling confident part. Most of my female clients and friends who have gotten divorced go through a similar phase: You have a renewed sense of yourself. You want to feel sexy again. And you want to *have* sex again. Hang on to that feeling for dear life! Soon after my split, I remember reading an article by a French mom about how women, American women in particular, let their sexiness go once they became mothers. Jeez, you don't say. I know I'm not the only woman to feel that. One client told me that, as a married mother of three, she would walk around the city feeling virtually invisible. The world is full of invisible armies of moms who've given up. And now look at us, checking people out—on the subway, in line getting coffee, out at restaurants. We're looking at everyone differently, including ourselves.

The nice thing about dating after divorce is that you have more life experience to know what's important and what isn't. I can speak for myself and clients and friends that the stretch marks and the wrinkles and the cellulite simply don't matter. If you're feeling comfortable in your own skin and feeling fabulous in what you're wearing, which equals feeling confident and sexy, your date isn't going to be noticing those superficial things. Others don't notice our flaws (or what we see as flaws) like we do. We are our own worst critics. *You* are the only one holding you back. So, my biggest piece of advice yet: get naked and feel fantastic about it!

Your Perfect Wardrobe

The second-best thing to feeling fantastic naked is feeling fantastic with clothes on.

At this point, you've purged your closet. You've committed to treating yourself to something new. You've committed to resisting shopping for your fantasy life. You've even committed to not obsessing about your so-called imperfections. Now it's time to home in on your personal style so you know what to get to replace all the stuff that doesn't fit your new life. I'm going to show you how to find your true-to-you style again (or maybe you've never found it and now is the time) and how to find ways to make small style changes that feel big.

Because I'm telling you all my secrets, I'm also going to share with you my knowledge of how to create a perfect wardrobe. After more than twenty years of working in the fashion world, I'm going to tell you the fifteen essential pieces that every woman should have in her closet. Not the *Vogue* version of the fifteen essentials, because that's realistic for .0001 percent of the population (that's one in a million). I'm going to tell you the Alyssa Dineen version—me, stylist and editor for twenty-two years, working with real women as well as famous ones, women of every size and with varying budgets—about what really matters and is actually practical for a wardrobe.

If fashion doesn't come easy to you or you don't have as much time or effort to put into it as you used to, then my advice is to keep it classic and simple. It's time-consuming to keep up with fashion and trends. The nice thing is—now that we've reached a certain age, we're not trying to be someone we're not. Choose things that are right for your body type and lifestyle. We don't have to pretend we're going to wear those four-inch heels anymore. Or, if you are, then congratulations! The rest of us can relax into a simpler style.

Remember those days in college and early adulthood when you felt like you needed to dress like your friends? I think back to when I would wear styles that did not suit my personality or body type only so I could keep up with my trendy friends. It was so nice to finally fall into styles that truly suited me, albeit not until after my divorce. Better late than never! So, own your level of style savvy. You don't need to veer into trends anymore. Quality over quantity is always better.

Let me lead you through the process for assembling the perfect wardrobe for your life *now*.

Address your foundational pieces.

Do I sound like your grandmother? Yes, I do. But that lady knew what she was talking about. "Foundational pieces" are essential, and there's a reason they're called that. You want to feel good from your foundation. They are building how you're feeling from the inside out. Even if no one is seeing your undergarments, those pieces are defining how you feel about yourself. Chances are, after getting divorced, you're wearing a yellowed bra that is stretched out and the lace is torn. Or maybe it's so threadbare it now has lace where there was never lace before. I've been there. And there's an 80 percent chance that you're wearing the wrong size too. If there is one thing to treat yourself to during this time, it's a new bra—wait, make it three. I recommend going to a lingerie shop or the lingerie section at a department store and asking for a fitting. It's free and worth the few minutes of awkwardness having someone feel you up in a store. You will walk into every date and meeting feeling sexier and empowered knowing you have perfectly fitting, quality underwear on.

Create a First-Date Uniform (FDU).

Right before a first date is not the time to reinvent the wheel. Know your FDU and have it ready. It saves you the stress of having a sea of clothes on your bedroom floor before each date, only to settle on a dress that looked cute on you once but now looks like a weird old lady housedress so you fancy it up with a belt, but, man, that's not doing you any favors, but the hell with it because you're already late. Good luck with that date. Damned before you step out the door and not feeling confident at all.

It took a couple of months of dating for me to figure out I needed an FDU. I'm saving you the hassle of making those same mistakes. It's okay to repeat this outfit because your date has never seen you in it before. And you'll always know what you wore when you first met the person and won't repeat it for the second date. Because, trust me, you're going out on a lot of dates if you put your mind to it.

Here's a starter kit:

- Your new, perfectly-fit-to-you-and-only-you bra.
- An updated pair of jeans that fits just tight enough in the butt—the fabric should have a little bit of stretch but still enough structure to hold you in.
- A handful of sexy tops to alternate. But not too sexy! By this I mean you can show one area of skin—shoulders *or* a bit of cleavage *or* your back—but not all at once.

- Jewelry that complements and does not take away from your face or your outfit. If you're into layering necklaces, three is the magic number, and make sure there is spacing in between each one, half an inch or more. If you're wearing a big necklace, wear small earrings and vice versa.

- Shoes that are sexy, but also don't hurt you. What's *not* sexy is wincing when you walk in your shoes.

Choose shoes wisely.

This is important. You want to feel comfortable enough so that if your date goes well, you can take a leisurely romantic stroll. However, you don't want to take the comfort factor so far that your shoes could ever be called "sensible." And not something so "sexy" that you're wobbling. I was recently out to dinner, and I watched as a young woman, probably around thirty, wobbled to the table next to us on five-inch stilettos. She was with a guy around her age. This was clearly a first date, which was easy to spot by the awkward body language and getting-to-know-you questions. The wobbler got up to use the restroom, looking as though she could topple over any moment. People held their wine glasses as she teetered past them. I'm sure she was kicking herself for wearing those heels on a first date. How would she walk to the subway or even out to the sidewalk when they left?

Here is my recommendation for first-date-goers: a heel of one or two inches, three max, is good. A block or wooden heel is even better. And for the love of God, please do not wear a new pair of shoes that you haven't walked in before. Ankle boots in colder months or block heel sandals in warmer ones are totally sexy, confident-feeling and -looking, and empirically walkable.

Sole Mate?

These FDU details can truly make a difference as to whether you go on a second date. After a first date with someone I met online, I was pretty certain I'd see him again. He texted me later the next day to tell me he'd enjoyed meeting me, and he asked if I wanted to go out again. When I answered yes, he pressed me to tell him what I liked about him. I thought about it, not realizing in the moment how self-focused this question was, and replied, "You were very sweet when I was so nervous and made a huge effort to make me feel comfortable. . . . Oh, and you also wore good shoes." It was the first thing I'd noticed about what he was wearing when I walked up to him outside the café. So, are first impressions important? Of course. And what you're wearing is part of that first impression.

Complement, don't distract, with accessories.

Another word of advice for your FDU: during most dates, the person is sitting across from you and sees you from the waist up. This requires some attention to what I call *table-top dressing*. Your top and accessories take on a new importance as they're what is most on display. At the same time, you don't want your clothes to divert attention from you. You want your top and accessories to complement you in the most non-distracting way possible. A simple top and a statement necklace, for example. Or a more interesting top with minimal jewelry, like small stud earrings.

Update your eyeglasses.

If there's one thing that can age someone, it's the style of the eyeglasses they're wearing. This is something that I immediately take a look at when I work with a new client. However, it's something that a lot of people can be pretty stubborn about: "Who cares what my glasses look like?" or "I'm not going to spend money on new glasses." Meanwhile, we just went on a shopping trip to buy a whole new wardrobe!

My answers to these excuses: "Yes, people notice," and "Yes, it's worth spending money on." Chances are, if you haven't bought glasses in the last three to four years, you're wearing a dated, out-of-style frame. So, if you're starting a new life and a new look, you need to update your eyewear.

This doesn't have to be an expensive endeavor anymore thanks to companies like Warby Parker, Caddis Eyewear, and Look Optic. Whether you need readers or everyday glasses or even prescription sunglasses, there are many fashion-forward options that won't cut into the rest of your wardrobe budget. Ordering eyeglasses online is a viable option with great return policies and try-at-home options. Choose ten styles/colors and try them all on at home. Try on your current frames along with the bunch and ask yourself whether you would choose those frames again today. Be honest and be realistic. If the answer is no, don't hold back in buying new ones. It's worth the money to feel good in an updated pair. Pick your favorite pair and return the rest.

Archetypes of Style

Classic is always, well, classic. No one ever said, "That looks nice, but I wish it had a crazier silhouette." My point? When in doubt, keep lines simple, palettes neutral, and fabrics natural. It's a formula that won't fail. A basic palette of white, black, and gray can get you through any situation beautifully. Think about it: How can you go wrong with jeans and a white or gray T-shirt during the day and black jeans with an oversized white button-down and some gold jewelry for a dinner out? Trick question, because you can't go wrong. You can see a woman wearing that outfit in 1960, 1990, or today (maybe with a different haircut). It's as Audrey Hepburn as it is Brooke Shields as it is Michelle Obama.

Having said that, we can't all be Audrey or Brooke or Michelle. And to be fair, "The Classic" doesn't inspire all of us. You might be reading about The Classic, thinking, *Well, that sounds great . . . for someone else.* Fair point.

So, I've come up with five additional over-the-age-of-thirty-five style archetypes. Maybe you will identify with one of these, or a few of them, and they will inspire you to try a new look. Maybe you'll bounce between a few. The point is: play, try, experiment, and see what fits.

Type: Breezy and Dreamy

I am bohemian but not broke, and as long as it's flowy and floral, I will run through any meadow with you and make flower crowns.

Poster Child: Liv Tyler, Nicole Richie

Dream Designers: Ulla Johnson, Zimmerman, Matta

Real Life: Free People, Anthropologie, Mango

Style: Bohemian types always seem so comfortable in whatever they're wearing. Not in a "I'm wearing sweats" kind of way but a "comfortable in my own skin and owning whatever ensemble I throw together" kind of way. Jewelry always plays an important role in Breezy and Dreamy's life, such as layering beaded necklaces along with fine gold chains, or stacking small bracelets, and the occasional pair of oversized earrings. She also carries an oversized bag—suede in fall/winter and crocheted in spring/summer. B&D prefers muted colors and natural fabrics. Summer is her favorite season, when she wears cutoff jeans on repeat and a bikini top under her gauzy shirts instead of a bra.

Warning: If she's not careful, this look can start to lean more to Grateful Dead groupie than boho chic.

How to pull it off: Wear long and/or flowy dresses with boots in fall/winter and sandals in spring/summer. Layer necklaces and delicate bracelets. Think cutoff denim, gauzy tops or tunics, caftans, and fringed suede.

Type: Rock 'n' Roll Mom

My teenage kids think I dress too young for my age, but I don't care.

Poster Child: Gwen Stefani, Zoe Kravitz

Dream Designers: Isabel Marant, Saint Laurent

Real Life: Zara, Urban Outfitters, some Target brands, secondhand and vintage stores

Style: The RNR Mom will be wearing all black (with maybe a camo print thrown in for good measure) whether she's attending her child's school play or with her friends for a night out. She always digs a motorcycle jacket but in an everyday, mom-of-two-kids kind of way—not a jumping-on-the-back-of-a-Harley kind of way. If RNR Mom wears a dress, it's definitely with boots. She most likely was not rock 'n' roll at all when she was younger, but now the RNR Mom is owning the look.

Warning: Although she doesn't care about dressing in a young and reckless kind of way, she can sometimes push it too far with her low-cut shirt, too-tight leather pants, and disheveled hair.

How to pull it off: Wearing all black is your bible, but with gray and white broken-in tees layered under whatever you're wearing—or better yet, a concert tee. Black jeans are easy to find, and these days, fake leather moto jackets are also easy to come by. Think concert T-shirts, leather or vegan leather pants and jackets, metallics, camo prints here and there, and motorcycle boots and jacket.

Type: Puffy Sleeves Don't Scare Me

The dresses I wear may be referred to as *frocks*, and I love an after-work cocktail with friends before going home for the night.

Poster Child: Tracee Ellis Ross, Busy Philipps, Zooey Deschanel

Dream Designers: Tracy Reese, G. Label

Real Life: Anthropologie, ModCloth, Rent the Runway

Style: I'm speaking to the prissy—and I mean that in a good way—hipsters of the world here. This woman loves her femininity and isn't afraid of ruffles, even some lace. Puffy Sleeves mostly wears skirts and dresses but more structured than B&D, as long as she can hop on her bike. She occasionally wears jeans, but they are high waisted and with some pops of color or a print and always with a low-heeled shoe. Never with sneakers. She only wears sneakers with a dress. Puffy Sleeves hates being called "quirky" even though it describes her perfectly.

Warning: She can sometimes go overboard on the quirky look. It's a look that is well served by being balanced.

How to pull it off: Rent the Runway could be your best friend since you like to change it up a lot and don't like to be seen in the same ensemble too many times. Think puffy sleeves, of course, eyelet, large floral prints, wide-leg pants, and block heel shoes.

Type: Sexy Nerd

Architectural and structured, I look like I run an art gallery in Berlin.

Poster Child: Issa Rae, Iris Apfel

Dream Designers: Marni, Prada, Acne Studios

Real Life: Zara, COS, The Real Real

Style: The architectural clothing type is into both form and function. You won't catch Sexy Nerd in anything constricting or overtly sexy. She likes black and white and bright colors. She can pull off a kooky necklace like no other and will rock a pair of lace-up flats with a dress without looking dowdy. Sexy Nerd looks like she spends a lot of money on her clothes even if she doesn't. But you're never thinking about that anyway because she always looks so put together and cool. Give her a structured handbag—big or small—and she's thrilled.

Warning: She may rely too much on her clothes to define her personality.

How to pull it off: You can always be keeping an eye on Zara's latest pieces as well as shopping at COS for a much-less-expensive-than-Prada way to achieve this look. Think textures, metallics, bright colors, and clean lines.

Type: The Curated Creative

I wake up every morning and always prefer jeans over anything else, and I secretly love wearing a fleece. However, I love and appreciate finer things—well-tailored pieces, a perfectly blended martini, that sort of thing—but never in a snobby way.

Poster Child: Angelina Jolie, Anh Duong

Dream Designers: Armani, Celine

Real Life: Everlane, Quince, The Real Real

Style: The CC is not boring. She is similar to The Classic, but she surprises you by splurging on a very cool designer top or dress. She throws on a great-fitting pair of jeans in the ideal wash along with a perfect T-shirt or blouse, and she's always the most stylish person in the room. The CC buys two pairs of perfect jeans (versus eight *meh* ones), and she wears them for five years or more until she needs to either update them or they get too worn in. And then she wears them to garden, paint, or hike. The CC invests in some great pieces that she wears over and over again but somehow no one notices. She always makes them look fresh. She can embody bohemian and puffy sleeves but in a downplayed way.

Warning: The CC can easily get lazy and not update her wardrobe enough or start wearing her fleece too often.

How to pull it off: Focus on high-quality timeless pieces that will last. Splurge on jeans if nothing else. Think cashmere, quality cotton, and wool, crisp shirts, and tailored pants.

Are You Ready for *The List*?

I belabored this list, checked and rechecked it, ran it by all of my fashion friends, and I think I've come up with the most edited version of essential pieces every woman should own. I'm talking about the pieces you should own, no matter your archetype. No matter your age. No matter your budget. If you have anxiety about investing in clothes, buy each piece as you can, as your budget allows. These are classic pieces. The wrap skirt is not going anywhere. It will be there when you are ready for it. After all, this wouldn't be much of an essentials list if the items on it fell out of fashion by next spring. I've listed these in order of importance so that you can go piece by piece and add to your wardrobe mindfully, at your own pace.

Fifteen Essential Pieces That Every Woman Should Have in Her Closet

A) A pair of dark denim, straight-leg jeans

I found mine at a designer discount store and have been wearing them for four years. They are timeless. They can go with your ankle boots for dates and meetings or your white weekend sneakers and a sweatshirt for a classic casual look. Look for contrast stitching so they don't look like jeggings.

Just make sure: These are fairly simple and clean looking. In other words, no major whiskering, holes, raw hems, or a flare. Those details aren't necessarily bad things, but they aren't for this pair of staple jeans for your wardrobe.

B) A pair of black slim or straight-leg jeans

No matter your size or style, everyone can use a black straight or skinny jean. I love that I can throw these on during the day with a T-shirt and white sneakers or dress them up to go out to a nice dinner with a blouse or my white, boyfriend-style button-down. They should be a dark black wash with a clean hem. They can be a cropped version too.

Just make sure: These don't have rips or holes so you can dress them up for meetings or evening events.

C) White cotton button-down

I'm talking about a quality cotton, boyfriend-style (i.e., no darts) button-down. Think Oprah Winfrey here or a character in a Nora Ephron movie. Wear it crisp and tucked into black trousers with layered gold necklaces, or slouchy and untucked with jeans and sandals. This should be quite oversized, no matter your body type, but be sure what you're wearing on the bottom offsets that by being slim and not oversized. Always a winner.

Just make sure: This is made of 100 percent cotton.

D) Black cashmere V-neck sweater

People get nervous when I say *cashmere*, because it can be pricey, but these days you can get fairly inexpensive cashmere at stores like Uniqlo and Everlane. It elevates your sweater game immediately. It shouldn't be too fitted—more of a slouchy mood. Typically this should be worn on its own without a T-shirt or camisole under it, which gives it a cleaner, classic look. If you like this look and find a good version of the sweater, get one in gray too. And maybe navy.

Just make sure: This doesn't have a tight ribbed band at the waist, which makes the style more conservative (and dated).

E) A pair of black ankle boots

These can be in suede, matte leather, or vegan leather. Be sure to try them on with dresses and skirts before you decide to keep them. They should hit you at a good place on your ankle that is flattering with non-pants. Avoid a heel that's too high—you need to be able to walk in them for work and dating. They can even have a flat sole.

Just make sure: They aren't shiny. Shiny leather ankle boots tend to look cheap.

F) A white sneaker for weekends

The style of the white weekend sneaker changes over the years, but it's been around forever so it's worth spending the money. I love that the trend has stuck around to wear them with skirts and dresses.

Just make sure: You get the flat-soled, lace-up kind. Not an athletic-looking one and risk looking like an '80's working-girl commuter, or one with no laces, which isn't timeless.

Fashion Speak

"A white sneaker" is fashion speak for "a pair of sneakers." I don't mean only one sneaker with you hopping on one foot; I mean two. People in the industry also call a pair of pants "a pant," and we call lipstick simply "lip."

G) Three well-fitting T-shirts in gray, white, and navy
This seems like something you would already have, but it's surprising how many women wear the wrong kind of T-shirts. And, by "wrong," I mean unflattering or ill-fitting or both. The right T-shirts will hit you at the right place at your shoulder and also your waist. Too soft equals shapeless in six months. Too thin equals bra-bulge revealing. Stay away from cap sleeves as this pretty much only works for girls under twelve. A U-neck or a scoop neckline is ideal. Wear these on their own with jeans or shorts or a skirt. Or layer under a blazer with jeans to up your T-shirt game a bit (see below).

Just make sure: They are a quality cotton or cotton blend. Also that they are not a shrunken T-shirt, which also only looks good on tween girls.

H) A black turtleneck
No matter your size, budget, or career, you need a good black turtleneck. You will wear it so much more than you think: with jeans and sneakers, tucked into a skirt, underneath your blazer, with a statement necklace to a party. It can be ribbed or not, and it can be either an actual sweater or a cotton/modal/lycra turtleneck.

Just make sure: The turtleneck is either fitted or slouchy—not in between.

I) A black blazer

I always wear a blazer when I want to feel like a badass, whether in an interview or on a date. And a blazer can fit both situations. I prefer to wear my blazer over a T-shirt in a sort of rock 'n' roll way. Or you can wear it over your white button-down, but do so with light-wash jeans to make it not so corporate. It can be a straight wool or a blend. And if you're buying more than one, the second one could be something exciting like suede or velvet or a tuxedo style.

Just make sure: This blazer is not the Brooks Brothers version. It shouldn't have prominent darts and should either be slightly oversized or shrunken.

J) Jean jacket

Think classic, hitting at the waist or hips. It should be slightly worn and could even have some shredded areas. Hardware can be copper or silver. Not too loose where you'll get lost, but not too tight that you can't button it.

Just make sure: It has the right wash of blue denim—not a flat blue. It can have fading or bleaching or be a dark denim.

K) Mid-length skirt

It should be mid-calf or just below the knee in length. It could be a print or a solid, whatever is going to be more versatile for you personally. Consider a wrap skirt for this. What I love about a wrap skirt is that the right one will fit you, no matter what. Whether you go up or down in weight, it will always be there for you. Wear it with your sandals or your white weekend sneakers and a T-shirt or your white button-down.

Just make sure: This should be a fabric and pattern that are versatile—for example, not in velvet (too dressy and wintry) or linen (too easily wrinkled and summery).

L) Light blue button-down

This shirt should fit the same way your white button-down does, only with a gauzier material. You should be able to wear this with a pair of shorts, tied at the waist with your wrap skirt, with jeans, and even with your blazer.

Just make sure: It's a light blue, preferably a washed-in light blue—not an in between "corporate" blue, dark blue, or navy. If it's striped, the stripes should be small, not wide.

M) A black or neutral sandal

For spring/summer, this should be a flat leather or suede sandal that will last. I've had some of my leather sandals for more than ten years and still wear them. I get sick of them before they fall apart. When in doubt, stick to a two-strap style, whether crisscross or parallel.

N) A black suede pump

A quality sleek pump can make an outfit. This can be worn with jeans out at night, with your wrap skirt to work, and of course can even be worn with a dress to a fancy party. And just like not wearing white after Labor Day or not wearing navy and black together, not wearing suede in summer is an old, dated rule, so consider these pumps suitable for every season.

O) A versatile black leather handbag

A bucket bag is your best bet. It's classic and can fit a decent amount of stuff. It could also be a saddlebag style or a simple crossbody style, which is forever in fashion.

Ask Alyssa

Q: I am on a tight budget and can't afford to buy many, if any, new clothes. Do you have any suggestions?

A: There are always ways to make yourself feel fresh. Any of my key pieces can be bought at stores like Target and TJ Maxx as well as secondhand at resale and consignment stores. And if you're not in the mood or not able to go shopping, do something on a small scale to freshen your look: get a haircut and/or a blowout, get your nails done, or buy a pair of new earrings. Also, keep in mind that you can acquire the essential pieces one at a time, as you are able, and build from there.

Fashion Math

Great. So, you've got your wardrobe. Now I'm going to break it all down for you. Many people will tell you that fashion is not math. And many people would be wrong. Here's what I mean:

C + A + I + E + O = First date coffee

J + B + C + F = Second date walk in the park

L + A + M = Saturday date to the museum

H + K + N = From work to a drinks date

A Note on Color

I realize the essentials include a lot of black. And that's not just because I'm a New Yorker. Black is a great color for your essentials, and I'll explain why. Think of it like

*fashion*MATH

FIRST DATE COFFEE

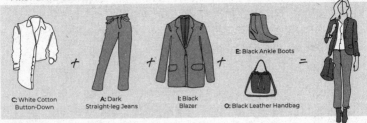

C: White Cotton Button-Down + **A:** Dark Straight-leg Jeans + **I:** Black Blazer + **E:** Black Ankle Boots **O:** Black Leather Handbag =

SECOND DATE WALK IN THE PARK

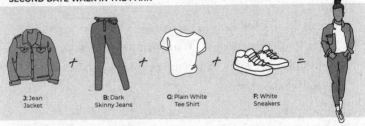

J: Jean Jacket + **B:** Dark Skinny Jeans + **G:** Plain White Tee Shirt + **F:** White Sneakers =

SATURDAY DATE TO THE MUSEUM

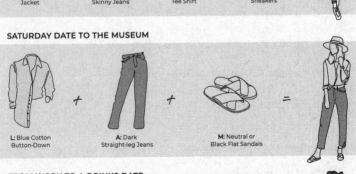

L: Blue Cotton Button-Down + **A:** Dark Straight-leg Jeans + **M:** Neutral or Black Flat Sandals =

FROM WORK TO A DRINKS DATE

H: Black Turtleneck Sweater + **K:** Neutral Mid-Length Skirt + **N:** Black Suede Pumps =

buying a new sofa. You want one in a neutral tone to last the test of time, and then you can brighten it up with pillows that can be replaced periodically. Start with a neutral palette and work up from there. I am not suggesting you only wear black, gray, and white for the rest of time. These are everyday basics, and, of course, add color if that makes you happy. In keeping with the sofa analogy, your "throw pillows" can be some interesting jewelry, a cool belt, or shoes with a print.

Tailor if Necessary

As a stylist, I have always had pieces of clothing tailored or altered to fit perfectly (that is, when I make the time). The time, effort, and money are worthwhile if they mean you'll wear an item instead of letting it sit in your closet. The problem with fast fashion and even high-end, long-life pieces is that they are made to fit a general audience. If you have a long torso or a short one, or long legs or short ones, long arms or short ones, you may not fall into these general sizes. I wish there were an easier solution, but until then, there is the tailor. If you find a piece that is right in every way, except the sleeve length is too long, paying for tailoring is the answer that will save you from months (or even years) of searching for the exact right thing.

The essentials are here to help you simplify your style and decision making. I want to reemphasize that these pieces work for all ages, body types, and budgets. You no longer have to have that teenage closet full of stuff that ends up strewn on your floor. You can be more stylish with fewer pieces that are higher quality.

Style Your Look Cheat Sheet

- If you're feeling comfortable in your own skin and feel good in what you're wearing, no one is going to notice superficial issues like weight, wrinkles, and stretch marks.
- Have fun trying on clothes, but actually buy clothes that fit your real life, not your fantasy life.
- Purchase quality, well-fitting undergarments, and feel good from your foundation.
- Create a first-date uniform (FDU) so you always have an outfit ready that you know looks and feels good.
- Choose shoes that are somewhere between sexy and sensible, and be sure on a date not to wear a new pair of shoes you've never worn before.
- Balance accessories: A simple top can be paired with a bold necklace or a more interesting top with minimal jewelry.

- Update eyewear. Old frames can age you.
- Explore your archetype of style, and have fun delving deeper into your fashion identity.
- Work on gradually building your wardrobe with the fifteen essential pieces.
- Mix and match your essential pieces for almost any event.
- Get items tailored when necessary.

3

Style Your Bio

The Importance of the Dating Bio

When my former roommate CSF (Cool Single Friend) first helped me put a profile up on Tinder, her opinion was: "Women don't need a bio. Men don't read them anyway." While that was probably and depressingly true in the early days of Tinder, I learned after a few months that I needed to write *something*.

Right away I noticed a difference: I was actually getting matches. A lot of them. I also started noticing how I read everyone else's bio and definitely responded more to ones that were humorous or interesting. And then I realized that I wasn't even swiping on anyone who hadn't written anything. If the person couldn't even spend ten minutes to write a bio, how serious was he about dating? I started out simply listing my interests:

> Yoga, tennis, running, skiing and snowboarding, my kids, my friends, wine and cheese. Not necessarily in that order.

Sure, I got matches and messages from that. But it tells as much about me as any active, city-dwelling, divorced mom. However, when I rewrote it to include more personal, unique things about myself, I matched with many more people, and more people messaged me based on my expanded bio. I kept adding and editing, and on one of the apps that allowed for more than five hundred characters, it eventually ended up like this:

> *I was raised to be modest, so talking about myself doesn't come naturally . . . but here goes: I'm restarting my career as a stylist and now art director. I'm finding myself rediscovering old interests I had deprived myself of—snowboarding and skiing, tennis, making out ;) working out, attempting to meditate, craft projects with my kids, and road trips. Music taste ranges from the Smiths to Led Zeppelin to Marvin Gaye to Beyoncé to Biggie Smalls. Favorite all-time TV show: Six Feet Under (I know, I know, that ages me, so be it). Don't ask me to name my favorite movie. Too hard.*

Favorite all-time travel experience: Going to Nairobi to do work there with a dear friend and live with locals. Gave me a perspective and experience of a lifetime.

Let me turn my critical eye on my own bio. Here's what works: It appeals to a lot of different music tastes, and it includes many different hobbies and interests. Here's what doesn't work: It's a bit humble braggy, along with listing off interests (telling) instead of telling a story (showing). It also invited a slew of sexual propositions with my "making out" comment. I took that phrase out pretty quickly.

Bios are part psychology, part art, zero rocket science. You can do this. You can create a bio that is eye-catching, authentic, fun. If you're reading this book, that means you're putting yourself out there, and you're at least somewhat committed to or interested in online dating. The more personal, the more honest, the more genuine your bio is, the better it will be and the more people you will attract. You will also be saving yourself time and headaches by not pretending to be someone you're not and matching with people who aren't right for you.

Ask Alyssa

Q: I'm worried about using my real name on the apps. What do most people do?

A: This is all about your level of comfort. At first, I only used initials, but once I felt more comfortable online, I used my real name. If you don't want to use your name because you don't want friends or family or coworkers to know you're online dating, then stop right there. Because everyone online dates now. My clients range in age from twenty to eighty years old and all walks of life. That being said, if you are concerned about it, initials are totally fine.

Ease up on the pressure to write the perfect bio. In fact, your first sentence can be, "I'm not a writer." You don't need to be. What you need to be is honest and sincere. I actually have clients who *are* writers and still have trouble writing about themselves. Enlist a trusted friend to help you. Gone are the days when you had to hide that you were online dating, since roughly 90 percent (maybe a slight exaggeration) of the population has at least tried it. Choose a friend to help you, someone who knows you inside and out and what you want in a partner. Then, if you stick to the guidelines below, you will stay in the safety zone.

What to Do in Your Online Bio

Write something . . . anything!

I can't tell you how many profiles I still see that have noth-ing written in their bio section. It's a common issue, but I can't overstate how damaging it is to the amount of matches you could be getting. Most people, me included, won't even consider a potential match if the person hasn't written anything at all. No bio suggests that the person is uninterested in online dating, thinks he or she is better than having to bother writing a description themselves, or they are hiding something (for example, they are mar-ried). My long-term partner I met online had a résumé as his bio—that's not what I would recommend, but it did tell me some things about him: that he traveled for work and that he had kids who lived a train ride away. Definitely bet-ter than nothing at all.

Pretend you're starring in your own biopic—
don't be afraid to brag a little.

In other words, be the most Hollywood glowing version of you. Don't create a character based on what you think oth-ers are looking for; be true to who you are by shedding light on your best traits, and you'll attract the right person into your life. One thing I often come across while work-ing with clients on their bios is the feeling that they don't want to say nice things about themselves for fear they will be perceived as boastful or full of themselves. I don't mean to sound cynical, but that's what you're supposed to do on a dating app. You're selling yourself. You're marketing yourself to others. You select the most flattering photos of yourself, right? Then why wouldn't you select the most flattering facts about yourself as well? You can do it in a way that doesn't sound braggy.

One of my clients, Barbara, was looking to match with other women. She was a lawyer by profession, but during one of our discovery sessions, she mentioned to me that she was really into cooking and had even written a cookbook. When I asked if we could include that in her bio, she immediately said, "No, I don't want to seem like I'm showing off." I told her that I thought most people would be thrilled to be with someone who was a great cook. I convinced her that I would word it in a way that did not sound like she was full of herself. Barbara agreed, and she said later it was something that most of the women she matched with responded to.

Show that you're human.

This may be the most important thing I say in this entire book. The clients and friends with whom I have worked over the past four years and who have been the most successful at online dating—in other words, those who met a long-term partner and in general met nice people through online dating—are the ones who show a softer, more un-guarded side of themselves. I'm not saying this means di-vulging that your father abandoned your family when you were a child. I am saying to show, in some way, that you're human like everyone else. Show a side of yourself that knows your flaws and can laugh at yourself.

Always stay positive. But in a normal, human way.

You don't need the perkiness of a sixteen-year-old cheer-leader. We all have ups and downs, likes and dislikes. How-ever, focus on the positive and leave the rest for later on. Dating bios are no place for anger and bitterness.

Include specifics.

Details add flavor to any story. Differentiate yourself from other foodies or avid readers by sharing your favorite dish or the specific books you've been reading lately. Do this in a non-braggy way—and this is a tricky line to balance. Be careful not to sound pretentious.

For example, instead of saying, "I love to read," men-tion the last three books you read, and be sure to include that cheesy beach read and maybe follow up with "Don't judge."

Talk about a recent trip you took, but include more de-tails than "Just got back from Italy." Instead, something like this: "Just had the best pasta of my life (orecchiette with broccoli) at a place in Puglia that might not have a restaurant license." Or better yet: "I just attempted to re-create a recipe from the best meal of my life in Puglia. It was a spectacular failure, and now I'm even more moti-vated to get back there!" As tempting as it is, talking about your travel exploits can come off as pretentious. Try to buffer it with a bit of self-deprecation.

Test your tone.
When you add travel or an expensive hobby into your bio, make sure you work it in without sounding like a jerk. So, instead of bragging about all the places you've been or your favorite ski resort, try describing a favorite meal you ate or museum you visited while on a trip or a particular experience while doing your hobby. You want to convey that you're an adventurous person—you do not want to brag that you've visited fifty countries. The point isn't out-doing someone, it's attracting people who are interested in the same things you are.

Be proud of your accomplishments, but mention them with a bit of humility. Or if you acknowledge that you sound a little bit douchey, it takes the sting away.

Here's a good test for your bio. Write a draft, then read it while pretending it was written by someone else. Would you date this person or does this person sound like a pre-tentious asshole? There's your answer.

Pick your words carefully, and tweak as necessary.

Jonathan was a client who reached out to me because he was hardly matching with any women. He couldn't understand why. He thought he was doing a pretty good job of representing himself. I had Jonathan send me his profile so I could take a look. His photos were decent but his bio . . . yikes. It had a line in there about a "dark past." Um, Jonathan, what do you mean by that? It turned out he was referring to his mother tragically passing away when he was only a teenager. I told Jonathan it came across more like a bodies-in-the-basement situation. He had no idea anyone could read it that way until I pointed it out. We lightened the tone, and he texted me that same night, shocked at what a difference it made so quickly. He almost instantly matched with more women. Point being: small changes, big rewards.

Another client, Wesley, came to me after a few months of online dating. He told me over the phone that he wasn't matching with many women. He also said that he wasn't attracted to the women he was matching with and that they didn't seem to be his type. I took a look and immediately saw his mistake. Wesley was into skateboarding, vintage T-shirts, had a vast record collection, and was a DJ on weekends for fun. Those aren't at all negative things, but he was coming off as way "too cool." He was most likely alienating women from even swiping right, never mind actually messaging him. I confessed that I, too, would not have swiped right on him, feeling that his hipster ways would make me feel uncool and inadequate in comparison. Although he had cool hobbies and an extremely cool style, in reality he was simply another divorced single dad who wanted to find love. We adjusted Wesley's bio to sound more approachable while still including the things he enjoyed.

Don't be afraid to get a little weird or step outside the mainstream.

Instead of using clichés and overused phrases, think about what makes you different from the rest. Are you learning to speak Hebrew? Do you collect succulents? Did you take welding classes in college? It's important to find the most unique things about yourself to talk about. I was once told on a first date that nearly all women on dating apps say they do yoga. I was one of millions apparently. It didn't make my profile stand out, that's for sure.

Mention deal-breakers.

Take time to reflect on who you are and what your needs and boundaries are. There are many things that can—and should—be negotiated in relationships. And, of course, you don't want to sound negative. However, don't be scared to mention any deal-breakers, such as smoking or children, or children who smoke! Or, these days, your political views. Most of the time, these can be accounted for in the stats, but if these are *really* important to you, definitely state them in the bio as well.

Get the conversation started.

Encourage people to contact you by including a call to action near the end of your bio. Consider adding a question to help break the ice or include something along the lines of "Interested? Send me a message and let's chat!" Or it could be that you list your favorite songs of 2020 and end with "What are yours?" It could be something even more specific to you and inviting questions about that. Such as, "I graduated college in 1995. Where were you in life in 1995?" or "Highs and lows of 2020? Mine were . . ." Remember to customize your call to action so it expresses your unique personality.

Let your writing make a good impression.

You don't need to be an amazing writer to create a great profile, but do check your spelling and grammar before you click submit. Wait until you see all the *your/you're* and *they're/their/there* mistakes out there in dating land! You do not want that to be you. The time and effort you put into your profile will show and be well received by others. If you don't trust that you know the difference between "effect" and "affect," enlist a grammar-nerd friend to read it and give you honest feedback.

What *Not* to Do in Your Bio

Lie about your age.

> *"I'm actually sixty-three, but I feel like I'm fifty-three, and my friends say I look much younger than I am :) I'm newly single and ready to mingle!!! I love going out with my girl-friends for margaritas, going to the movies, and I love my grandchildren more than anything!!!!"*

First rule of thumb: don't lie about your age. It's not worth it, and when the truth comes out, it's pretty embarrassing. Aside from that, this bio seems good enough, right? Nope. At best this bio is lame and forgettable, and at worst, all those exclamation points come across as slightly un-hinged. Don't let exclamation points stand in for your personality. Additionally, this content tells the reader no more about you than any other sixty-something, American, divorced woman with grandchildren.

Overuse emojis.

Okay, so let me get this straight: You have a dog? Or you like dogs? You like to kiss? Or you wear lipstick? You like the beach? Or maybe that means vacations? You like avocados? You like a cocktail? Or maybe you like to party? You like music and you're looking for love? Or you and your dog eat avocados when you go to Tulum and listen to high-pitched music and then you drink something with rum and put lipstick on each other?

I love an emoji as much as the next millennial, but a parade of them is not a bio. This may have been cute and original ten years ago, *maybe*, but now it's plain annoying to decipher. Who has the time? I think I'll swipe left, thanks.

Draw attention to the fact that you're online dating.

> *"Never thought I'd have to do this [insert comment about wife leaving and/or expecting to meet someone in person], but here I am. I'm looking for an honest, loyal person to enjoy life's simple pleasures."*

No one thinks they are going to have to online date. Absolutely no one. And we all feel we shouldn't have to on some level. But here we all are. Mentioning this is counterproductive and makes everyone else feel somehow inadequate that they are online dating.

Focus on what you're not looking for.

> *"No douchey facial hair styles (e.g., the lamb chops, soul patch, or Flavor Saver), high maintenance egos, and guys who spend more than an hour a day at a gym.*

> *"First date nightmares: fancy wining & dining or a loud bar yelling in each other's ear"*

This bio is extremely negative. Very funny, but negative. I like her details, and she has a strong sense of what she doesn't like, but I want to hear more about what she *does* like.

Have a chip on your shoulder.

"Smart, successful entrepreneur who isn't looking for a frivolous fling or a prince charming to sweep me off my feet. I can take care of myself just fine. I have two grown children who are independent and live on their own. I'm also a triathlete but I like a good martini and steak once in a while. Looking for a guy who has similar interests and is also at a point in his life where he doesn't need a woman to take care of him."

I'm not sure why this person feels the need to prove something to me. Also, why so angry? There's a way to list accomplishments—and by all means, do!—without sounding negative. Also, this type A person doesn't sound like she would be much fun (which actually isn't the case—I know her). She simply comes across as a righteous stick-in-the-mud in the sentences she's written.

Be judgy.

"I think video games are evil—I want my future kids to be cut up and bruised from climbing trees and riding bikes, not

> *fat-assed in front of the TV being conditioned for army*
> *drone piloting. That goes for my partner as well."*

Said like a nonparent if I ever heard one! Although she has some sass and personality—this is anything but boring—she comes off as harsh and judgy. Plus, is *this* the first thing you want people to know about you?

Let the picture do the talking.

> *"Need I say more?"* [These were the only words written
> with only one photo. The photo was the man in his tighty-
> whitey undies.]

I'm not making this up. I don't think I need to explain why this is not, by any stretch of the imagination, an appropriate bio.

Other Common Bio Foibles

"Life Story As Bio"

The "Life Story As Bio" person tells every detail of him- or herself in the written bio—this would be on the apps like Match and OkCupid that give you quite a lot of space to write, unlike the swiping apps. This person includes so much information that you feel like there's nothing else to know. You know all their children's ages, where they have lived over the past twenty years, as well as the three career paths almost pursued before stumbling on his or her current job. It's nice to tell some detail, but you don't need everything in one shot. And if it's too long, people will get bored and stop reading halfway down anyway. You want to leave some question marks so that your potential matches have something left to ask you about. If you do go a little long, be sure to at least keep it interesting. When in doubt, let friends read it and see what they say.

"Cocktails and Clubs"

The "Cocktails and Clubs" person names every favorite bar and restaurant and what drink to order at each place. That isn't telling much about you other than you like to go out drinking. And I'm sure there's more to you than that. Maybe partying with friends is your thing, but let potential matches get to know that on the first date. Also, all the photos are of C&C with at least one friend but usually two or three and always at night, and always partying. But more on that in chapter 4.

"Bitter About Life"

The "Bitter About Life" person is, well, bitter. About life. And this person doesn't hold back in the bio. Most of the time, it's about divorce or a recent relationship that ended badly. But sometimes it's a tone of overall anger about the person's lot in life. I've been there myself, and it's difficult not to tell the world that you're hurt and therefore angry. But please, don't.

We can't all be "loyal, kind, and funny."

If I had a quarter for every time I saw these adjectives while I was online dating or working as a dating coach, I'd be wearing nothing but Chloé and Isabel Marant for the rest of my days. This is a psychology lesson in and of itself. *Everyone*, and I mean 99 percent of people, think they're these three adjectives. And while I like to think we all could be, it simply can't be true. But more important, since everyone thinks this of themselves, they all want to write it into their bios. You will see, when you get out there, that if they haven't read this book, they probably use at least one of these characteristics to describe themselves. When everyone describes themselves as "Loyal, Kind, and Funny," those words cease to have meaning. Not to mention that it goes against my rules of getting weird and being unique. Think of some other more interesting and original ways to describe yourself. If you actually are these three things, try to think of another way to say it. Or go to Thesaurus.com. Seriously. As the editor of this book has told me again and again, the best way to describe something is to show, not tell.

"Funny" can mean so many different things to different people. Are you *Saturday Night Live* funny or Jerry Seinfeld funny or David Sedaris funny? Some clients like to think they're funny, but laughing at Jon Stewart does not make *you* funny. It merely means you appreciate funny. Don't say, "I'm funny." Try instead, "My Trump impression is possibly better than Alec Baldwin's. Just saying."

"Loyal" is another one of those terms that could have multiple contexts. Loyal to your job or to your friends? It could mean loyal to the town you grew up in. Or it could be "the big one": that you were loyal to your ex who then cheated on you. And again, *everyone* seems to think they are loyal in some way. So, don't say, "I'm loyal." Instead say, "I've had the same best friend since first grade."

"Kind." Now, "kind" is better than "nice," sure, but it's still boring. Don't say, "I'm kind." Explain that you've volunteered for your local ASPCA organization for the past nine years.

Once you're on the dating apps, you'll see what I mean about the repetitive phrases and words. I remember thinking that if I saw one more man whose profile said he was "self-aware," I was going to lose my mind! Always go back to the concept of including specifics if you feel yourself slipping into clichès or overused phrases. If you're not sure what phrases I'm talking about, see the list below. These are ten phrases and topics you'll see over and over again. Not only that, but, for the most part, no one should have said them in the first place.

Ten Phrases and Topics to Avoid in Your Online Dating Bio

1. **That you are "loyal," "kind," or "funny" (or all three!).** Look, you might very well be. But unfortunately, the world of online dating has made these three adjectives the most used of all adjectives. Ergo, they are starting to mean nothing.

2. **That you are "self-aware."** People who truly are self-aware know better than to say this.

3. **Mention that you're not divorced yet.** To me, this is something that can be discussed by text before you actually meet. I know a lot of people are dead set against dating someone who is only separated, but most people are agreeable as long as they understand where you are emotionally. You don't want to turn everyone away immediately without explaining your situation.

4. **That you're "not looking for hookups or one-night stands."** Don't waste the scant real estate of the bio sections. It's another overused phrase. In your stats section, you will have already made clear what type of encounter you're looking for.

5. **Trash-talk about your ex-boyfriend, ex-spouse, ex-anything.** You will seem bitter and judgy. Once you have perfect strangers thinking you need to move on, well, you need to move on.

6. **Anything about being "wealthy," "very fit," "attractive."** These are not the words of someone who is confident and self-assured. If you need to brag about how much money you have or how good-looking you are, you might need a therapist more than a date.

7. **That you're "drama-free" or "not looking for any drama."** Who is?

8. **That you are "new to this."** You can discuss this once you match with someone and are messaging. It does not need to be in your bio.

9. **Any reference to rehab or therapy or debt.** This may be a click too honest.

10. **That you "don't know what you're doing wrong," because you're "not matching with many people or getting many dates."** This is not sexy, and it comes off as a bit sad. You're not here for any pity dates.

Examples of Great Bios

Smart and to the point

> *I make it a point to find the time for doing the things I enjoy and spending the time with people whom I care about, and I absolutely refuse to become a slave to my job despite the NYC work ethic! I like people who have humor and wit, self-confidence but not narcissism, resilience, strength of character, and a willingness to learn. I prefer people who have been through some sh—t in life and pushed through it. In other words, I am not going to make your lemonade for you but I am happy to hear about how you made that lemonade!*

What I like about this bio is that the writer's voice comes through. She really tells something about herself in her bio, not by telling but by showing. We can tell she is a good friend and that she's intelligent and self-confident.

Quirky

> *If you are picky about what kind of coffee you drink, put your phone away during dinner, and prefer Coen Brothers over Steven Spielberg, I'm your girl (woman? person?). I'm also volunteering at my local library. If we hit it off, I might teach you the Dewey decimal system.*

This bio is nicely written and, well, quirky. I like that she ends with a really tempting call to action!

Sweet

> *I am a sensitive person who likes to take care of others. But not to the point of being a doormat! I volunteer at the Museum of Modern Art whenever possible because I'm a frustrated artist who became an ophthalmologist. I still love to see art and paint with my daughter whenever possible. Also, I love to spend time off walking through new cities: street art and checking out hole-in-the-wall coffee shops are my thing.*

This person is showing, not telling, that she is creative, smart, motivated, and a single mom. I like that she let us know about the very different sides to her personality.

Unique and funny

> *I disapprove of joining cults and cover bands. I approve of paid time off and karaoke. I discourage overindulgence and under-stimulation. I encourage playing with children and learning a second language. I like historical novels and trampolines. I am uninterested in vapid minds and reality TV. I am interested in witty banter and challenging repartee. Now what about you?*

I want to meet this person, don't you? Opinionated but definitely not boring. I also see all the many sides to this person's personality, and I want to know more. And, of course, a call to action is always a good thing.

Clever

> *Parallel parker extraordinaire, semiprofessional bathroom*
> *singer, never been in jail (except when playing Monopoly). I*
> *won't bore you with stories about my dog or my children.*

This is fairly simple, but again, it's going to get responses
because it's interesting and not your average information.
It's just enough weird, just enough funny, and well, just
enough.

Ask Alyssa

Q: I feel like all I do is work. I don't remember the last
book I read! For my bio, do I talk about my job
since it really is what I tend to focus on or do I mention those
hobbies I used to have years ago and haven't touched since?

A: A lot of people come to me and feel like they don't
have any interests or hobbies when in fact they do.
It can even be something as simple as "I like going for walks
in new neighborhoods with my dog" or "I read the *Times*
cover to cover every weekend." Dig deep, and I know you
can find some other interests. Alternatively, you can make a
joke out of it: "Trying to get to that bucket list of mine of
postdivorce activities."

Prompts

Now that a lot of the dating apps include prompts to answer (usually three prompts or questions), and in the case of Hinge, it replaces a bio altogether, you have to get creative about providing answers that include the most information about you as possible. There are usually up around fifty prompts—yes, almost too many to choose from!

Below are a few examples of the prompts you'll see. Even the blandest of these prompts can illicit an interesting response. It's a fun exercise to figure out how you can answer each in the most catchy way. If you're funny, be funny. If you're not, don't force it. But no matter what, you can make it interesting.

1. My mantra is . . .
2. Don't hate me if I . . .
3. Fact about me that surprises people . . .
4. Give me travel tips for . . .
5. I bet you can't . . .
6. I geek out on . . .
7. I get along best with people who . . .
8. I go crazy for . . .

Here's how I would answer the above prompts to get the most responses.

1. My mantra is . . . *Work hard and be nice to people.*
2. Don't hate me if I . . . *Nap instead of actually meditate. My intentions are there!*
3. Fact about me that surprises people . . . *I grew up vegetarian, became vegan in college, then fell in love with burgers in my late twenties. Now I'm somewhere between a pescatarian and a vegetarian.*
4. Give me travel tips for . . . *India.*
5. I bet you can't . . . *Paint a waterfall by watching a YouTube video.*
6. I geek out on . . . *Watching woodworking videos on Instagram.*
7. I get along best with people who . . . *Don't take themselves seriously, don't feel sorry for themselves, and treat others with respect.*
8. I go crazy for . . . *Warm apple cider donuts.*

Statistics

And then, of course, there are the stats the apps ask for. Things like height, body type, activity level, what level of schooling you've completed, hometown, religion, political leaning, whether you have or want kids, what type of relationship you're looking for, and so on. Depending on the app, these are given as a drop-down menu, a box to check, or choices to select. Some apps charge you to upgrade your account in order to narrow your selection to only people who fit your criteria. For example, if you know you definitely want someone who wants kids, you could narrow your selection to just those people and, therefore, would want to upgrade.

Height: If you are a male, you *must* fill this out or else that's all you'll be asked by women. Although women should fill it out too. And don't lie about it!

Body type: Don't exaggerate on this. It's always good to be up front.

Religion: Many people skip this because they don't want to be pigeonholed. For others, it's important that the person is the same religion they are.

Politics: This is obviously a hot-button item. Historically, sex, politics, and religion are all taboo. These days, it's too divisive an issue to leave blank. Most people want to know one way or another before they get into a conversation with someone.

Kids or no kids: Of course, if you feel very strongly either way, you definitely mark this one. If you think hard about it and feel that, for the right person, you would change your position, then skip this question. This can be a bigger conversation once you've dated. This is sometimes broken up into two different questions: 1) Are you open to having kids/

more kids with a new partner, and 2) Are you okay with someone who has kids already/or you have your own kids.

Journal into It

One way to look at writing your bio is to treat it as if you're writing in your journal. Try describing your life as if you're looking back on your life and retelling it to your grandchildren. Be honest and witty and specific. Try bragging about your life but without any ego—your grandchildren wouldn't want you to sound douchey. They would simply want the truth, *retold in an interesting way.* Remember that this is a work in progress. You can keep adding to your bio and edit as you go along. At some point, you may even be completely satisfied with it. Still, don't ignore it and let it get stale. Use your journal as a resource—refer back to old entries to get ideas about what you like and dislike and the interesting things you've done. Your bio, in essence, should be like a microcosm of your journal.

For me, my journal also played another important role in my bio. The pressure to write a bio and to sound interesting can bring up a lot of issues. If you've recently been through a divorce or other significant life change that has brought you to the precipice of online dating, then simply going to work, taking care of your kids, and sleeping well at night might be about as interesting as it gets and you're damn proud of yourself for that. So, how does that healthy, functioning, but "boring" lifestyle translate to a bio someone's going to swipe on?

One way I "developed" my bio, for my profile but also for myself, was to journal about what I wanted in my new, postdivorce life, and my intention to experience new things. In my journal, I wrote about wanting to travel. Not family vacation travel but out-of-my-comfort-zone travel. I wanted to see the world the way I had when I was young. I wanted to be blown away. I wanted to be scared and intimidated and humbled. I wanted to see my own life from the outside, from the perspective of a different culture. I wanted to eat food I couldn't find in New York (which isn't easy!). And I wanted to be inspired. Corny though it may sound, I wanted to find myself by escaping my world.

Now, keep in mind, I was on an extreme budget that hovered around $0, so it was not clear how this wild, life-changing adventure would happen. But I dutifully wrote my desire for it in my journal and manifested the hell out of it. I didn't pray exactly, but I would envision myself, backpack in hand, getting on an airplane, and flying to a far-away place. And, fine, at the time it could have been that I wanted to escape the hell of my divorce and get as far away as possible. But it was also that I wanted to get out of my New York City, first-world bubble and experience different foods, another culture, and maybe even some discomfort.

Close to a year after I first wrote about my Indiana Jones fantasy, I got a call from my friend Kate who was planning a trip to Kenya. She is a jewelry maker involved with a nonprofit called Women4Women (W4W) in Africa that supports women and their children, girls' education, and creating networks among entrepreneur designers like Kate and local craftsmen so that people can earn a living and provide for their families. Kate was going to Kenya to visit a metal-working studio for a potential partnership and to train women to make the jewelry in her line.

She had a proposal for me: She would hire me as her overqualified assistant. She needed help, she hated traveling alone, and she wanted someone who could assist in the work and design. Someone, say, who had experience as a stylist. Since I had my kids only half the time since the divorce, I was also more available than most of her other friends. Suddenly, my budget of $0 was not a problem. Next thing I knew, I was smooshed into a middle seat on a thirty-six-hour journey to Nairobi. And you couldn't have smacked the smile off my face.

My first day in Nairobi was so different from any other day in my life. After lunch—a traditional Kenyan meal made by one of the mothers who now worked with the director of W4W—we headed to see some of the girls perform in a musical. I marveled at the surroundings, so unlike any place I had ever been, the trees that looked like peacock feathers and the sound of horns honking constantly. I didn't think once about my stupid divorce.

The next day, we visited a sewing workshop in Kibera and met women who were taking beautiful printed fabrics and making bags and dresses like the ones they themselves were wearing while going about their normal day. I felt underdressed in my jeans and T-shirt. The seamstresses welcomed Kate and me into the small room with a corrugated roof and a few sewing machines to watch what they were making. At first, we stood awkwardly and quietly, observing the steady hum of their work. But soon we found a common language in fashion as they showed us how they made the dresses as well the stylish sandals they crafted from local leather.

After that, we walked into the Kibera slums to visit a metal worker in his studio. The artisan had a few men working outside at sanding wheels, grinding down the materials to use for his jewelry. We stepped inside another corrugated metal studio, this one with dirt floors. We were awed by the artisan's sketches that hung on the wall of pieces he'd designed and made by hand from brass, horn, and bone found locally around Nairobi. He and his crew made gorgeous rings and bracelets and necklaces. Kate knew immediately she had come to the right person to collaborate with on her designs. I learned more that day than I had on fifty fashion shoots.

The day after that, we set up a makeshift workshop in the program director's home to train the women who would make the jewelry Kate had designed. Many of the women had narrowly escaped the sex trade. Since I couldn't put into words any of the thoughts that ran through my head as I admired their courage, I did what I was getting good at: I got down to the business of fashion—in this case, accessories. Kate and I showed them a few beaded bracelet designs that they could make at home or at the studio to help them earn money and support their families.

The next day, we skipped fashion altogether. We toured downtown Nairobi, where we people-watched, ate street food, and went to the markets to buy gifts to take home to our kids. The energy, the conversations, the smell of burning trash mixed with delicous foods being cooked—it was cathartic. Transportive. As far from my life as I could get, almost as if I had been dropped on another planet. Throughout that day, I found myself about to cry. I wasn't sad, but they weren't tears of joy either. It was more like overwhelming emotion.

I came back home reenergized. It was good to get out of my New York bubble. Actually, that's a hell of an understatement.

So, what does that life-changing trip have to do with my online dating bio? Well, even if I couldn't put into words what the trip meant to me within the limitations of my online profile, I knew that I wanted to convey that I was someone who enjoyed travel, adventures, new experiences, different cultures. Someone who enjoyed getting out of her comfort zone. And I was looking for the same in a match.

Manifesting travel was for me a way to step outside of myself, beyond my immediate world. If you are feeling ho hum about your bio, consider travel, even if that simply means traveling outside your comfort zone and not literally to an exotic locale.

If I learned one thing from the COVID-19 pandemic, it's that travel doesn't have to be geographical. It can be driving to a new city or even a new neighborhood, experienced through new cuisines. It could be reading a travel memoir or a book written by an author from a place you've never been. Even watching *Jiro Dreams of Sushi* or *Eat Drink Man Woman* and preparing a meal from one of those countries.

In my opinion, travel, even experienced virtually, is a way to find out who you are—a way to get to know yourself better. Making connections with different cultures, foods, and people forces you to step outside of your personal bubble and feel a little lost, disoriented, not in charge or in control—it sounds like online dating at times! If you're feeling stuck when it comes to your bio, take a trip, remember a trip, journal about your intentions for a trip, and see what pops up. Doing cool things can make a great bio. Making a great bio can lead to cool things.

Style Your Bio Cheat Sheet

- Do include a bio. Don't let your photos do all the talking.
- The more personal, specific, and genuine your bio is, the better matches you will get. "Show, don't tell" with specific stories rather than listing hobbies or interests.
- Brag on yourself a little by sharing good things about yourself while also showing you're human and someone who can laugh at herself.
- Use a positive tone—no bitterness, judginess, trash-talking exes, or obvious chips on your shoulder.
- Pick your words carefully and tweak as needed—avoid clichés like "loyal," "kind," "funny," and "self-aware." Stand out by being original and sharing what's unusual about you.
- End with a call to action to get a conversation started.
- Edit your bio for grammar and spelling.
- Be creative with prompts and honest with stats.
- Journal as a way to dig deeper into your interests and develop your bio.
- Open yourself up to new experiences and travel, and see what you learn about yourself.
- Get feedback on your bio from a friend who knows you well and knows what you're looking for.

4

Style Your Selfie

Capturing the Real Me

There's a photo of me with my younger daughter that was taken the first summer of my single-dom. It's on my night table—the first thing I see every morning when I wake up and the last thing I see before I go to sleep. It's in a simple silver frame that was probably a graduation present from a million years ago. For all intents and purposes, the picture is unremarkable, but to me, it's everything. That summer carried with it a cloud of stress—a thunderstorm of anxiety might be more accurate—from my divorce, but that week I was relaxed in a way that I hadn't been in . . . forever.

My friend Emily had invited me and the girls to her beach house for a week. We arrived on a Monday in the late afternoon and pulled into the driveway. Emily's kids came running out to greet us, and in minutes, the whole gaggle of them ran down to the beach. I could see the ocean from the driveway, and I could smell the sweet, briny sea air. I felt a freedom I hadn't felt since I was twenty years old—the era in my life in which I would decide last minute to go camping with my friends, and we would leave the next morning. I had no one to answer to. I had no one who needed to know what I was doing. I could let my kids eat ice cream for dinner and stay up until midnight and no one would guilt me about why those were bad choices. I unpacked the car by myself, feeling for the first time what it meant to be a single mom. It wasn't all bad. On vacation at a friend's beach house, anyway.

Emily grabbed a bottle of rosé and two plastic cups, and we walked down to the water with a couple of chairs. The kids took turns driving a kid-sized, electric jeep up and down her unpaved street, an idyllic sandy road that ended at the beach. We watched them and chatted until it was close to dinnertime and we were almost out of wine. My younger daughter, always the more snuggly one, took a break from the fun, ran over to us, and curled up on my lap in the beach chair. Knowing I seriously needed to up my game with my profile photos, I was trying to be better about taking pictures when I was out with friends. It was an exercise I wasn't used to. I hadn't grown up in a world of constant photo-taking, and I would often go home after an event or a fun night out having forgotten to take a single photo, let alone a selfie. This time I remembered. I asked Emily to take a few photos of us, and she happily went to work. Up until that point, I'd hated photos of myself, but this one felt like the real me. Five years later, it remains one of my favorite pictures. I love it.

Let's deconstruct what I like about that photo. It bears repeating, because I think a lot of women feel this way: until this photo, a photo I really, truly liked of myself did not exist. I had tried hard to find one. But this one was different. I like how I'm the most me in photos with my daughters. I like how the beach breeze is blowing my hair in a cute, messy way (there's a reason photographers like to use fans on fashion shoots). I like that I have a smile that is genuine, as though I'm on the brink of laughing. I like that it's summer and my freckles have come out and my skin is glowing and healthy-looking. I like that my right eye squints a little more than my left. And I like that I'm wearing a sleeveless, gray, muscle T-shirt that shows off my new strong arms from all the boot camp classes I was doing. That photo was and still is my gold standard when I think of photos of myself.

Once I decided to venture into online dating, I scrolled through *all* my photos on my laptop to see if I had anything worthy of putting on a dating app. I didn't. Like most moms, all of my photos had my kids in it. Or my ex-husband. I had to start acting like a single woman and not like a married mom. I didn't want to look like a "hot mom." I wanted to feel like a hot woman. I had to up my photo game.

I was decidedly not into having my photo taken, mainly because I had barely a shred of self-confidence left before becoming single. But as I started feeling better about myself and slowly rediscovered my mojo, I got better at getting my photo taken and taking selfies. I practiced and practiced and practiced and oh how I practiced taking selfies at home. I also got better at remembering to ask friends to snap a photo of me when we went out to dinner together.

I asked my older daughter to take photos of me, too, since I felt the least self-conscious in front of her. This is something I suggest to a lot of my divorced clients. Your kids have no agenda with you and most likely don't know why you're even taking the photos. But they do know who the real you is, and they will make sure that's what they're getting. I actually got the hang of this photo thing after a few months. As I did, I kept switching out my old photos for new and better ones on the dating apps and got better and better response rates as a result.

Kids in Pics or Not?

A lot of newbies to the online dating world are wondering about this. And, like giving out your real number to people, it's all preference. Some people do not want their children anywhere near their dating profile. Some people put pics with their kids in them but block out their faces. And some are fine including their children in their profile. If you choose to include your kids, I don't recommend having them in more than one photo. It may give off the message that you're with your kids all the time and potential matches may think you're not available to go on dates. Even if that's the case, you probably don't want to discourage people from the get-go.

Photo Traps

As we all know, a photo speaks volumes. The flip side of that coin is that sometimes it sends an unintended message. Allison was a client of mine in her late fifties. She'd been single for a while since her divorce, and now she was ready for a serious relationship again. She didn't understand why she was only getting attention on the dating apps from men wanting sex and hookups.

I took a look at Allison's photos, which included a selfie of herself aiming a kiss at the camera and another of her out at night wearing a very low-cut dress. Those two photos were creating a profile that said, "I'm here for some fun." We replaced those two pictures with a mix of just-sexy-enough photos along with some active photos of her and her dog. Problem solved. She was matching and getting messaged by men who were much more aligned with what she was looking for.

Horrible and confusing profile photos abound on dating apps, no doubt because most people who are not in a creative industry (or under the age of thirty) don't really know what to look for in a photo or even what constitutes a "good photo." I have seen 18,000 selfies of men strapped into seat belts in their cars, a.k.a. "the car selfie." I have seen 14,000 photos of men holding a fish they caught. (This one stumps me—does every single guy go fishing as some kind of hazing into single-dom?) I have seen 10,000 selfies of men staring slack-jawed at the screen of their phone while they take a selfie in their bathroom mirrors, usually with bad lighting to boot. I have seen 7,000 selfies of glistening, tank-topped men in their gym. I have seen 3,000 pics of men on a surfboard for the very first time in their lives. I have seen hundreds of photos of men holding someone else's baby (yes, this is actually a thing). I don't recommend any of the above.

Ladies, we're not immune to our own photo missteps. Women have their own set of issues with profile photos:

the yoga selfie, the twelve-girlfriends-in-one-shot and you can't tell whose profile it is, the photo with the cropped-out ex because they don't have any photos of them without kids or ex-husbands, the blurry or bad-lighting shot, and, of course, the ten-year-old photo that looks nothing like the rest of the person's pics.

For whatever reason, we all gravitate to the same photo mistakes. As in your bio with "loyal, kind, and funny," you, too, will be pulled into these selfie and photo traps. You must resist! There's nothing wrong with a selfie, as long as you've practiced taking it five hundred times before putting it on your profile.

What Photos *Should* You Include?

This is my tried-and-true list of what needs to be included in every person's online dating profile:

1. *A headshot.* Or a waist-up shot that shows your whole face, looking at the camera, without sunglasses or a hat. And you must be smiling— or at least smiling with your eyes. This should almost always be your first/main photo.
2. *An active or hobby shot.* Whether you're a gardener, a painter, a runner, or you love

antiquing, you should have one photo of you doing something that you enjoy. Not only to show you're not a couch potato but to encourage people to ask you about said activity, which will start a conversation.

3. *A social shot.* This can be as simple as asking the waiter to take a pic while you're at dinner with a friend. Or it can be at a wedding or at a party with friends. Or it can be at a sports event with colleagues. Whatever it is, make sure it's a moment when you're having fun. These are the times when you have to remember to get those shots before you leave for the night.

4. *A full-body shot.* This is important, because many people won't even swipe if they only see shoulders-up shots of you. They want to know what the whole you looks like, and they definitely don't want any surprises. I realize this is unfortunate and maybe the whole world has turned into a Miss America pageant in the twenty-first century, but it's the reality of the world in which we live. Do with that what you will, but I know a lot of online daters won't meet with someone or even swipe right on someone with only headshots. By the way, this

full-body shot can also be the social or the active shot. That's a great way to work in a full-body shot without having to take an awkward full-body selfie.

5. *The just-sexy-enough photo.* I know, for some of you, this one will feel forced or uncomfortable. For others, you're thinking, *My whole profile is made up of sexy pics.* A nice balance should be your goal. In my opinion, there should be one photo in the group where you show a little skin and/or have an expression that is sexy. What makes a sexy expression? It's in the eyes. You have to be feeling sexy to look sexy.

6. *Dealer's choice.* Most apps have at least six slots for pictures, so fill them up. Pick whatever you'd like for the final one—this one can really show your personality.

Some apps ask for more photos. Again, as long as you have fulfilled 1 through 5 on the list, the others are up to you, but try to use all of the slots that are available. But do not include a picture of your cat or your nana's lasagna or the latest sunset pic you took. They want to see *you*.

Let's handle the things we know we can handle. You may have no idea of what to wear or how to date, but now you do know what six photos to include in your profile.

Caveat: If you have a photo that flies in the face of all these rules, but you still love it, then definitely use it. First, run it by a friend or someone who knows you well (and knows the difference between a good picture and a bad picture) to make sure you're not the only one who likes this photo.

Once you have your collection of photos selected for your profile, then look at everything together on your profile and see what's missing. Do you feel it's an accurate and complete representation of you? If not, what feels out of place? What's missing? How can you find a place to include what's missing either in your bio or your photos?

Pump Yourself Up

If you're taking photos specifically for your profile, let me break with convention for a second and give you some unusual advice. Bear with me. There's something you should do before having your photo taken, whether you are taking the photos or someone else will be taking them: get pumped up for your photo shoot.

Before public speaking, you would prep in some way to relax and take your anxiety levels down, right? So, why not for your profile pics? I'm talking about the stuff that has nothing to do with what you look like or the lighting or your head position. I'm talking about taking at least thirty minutes beforehand that is only for you. Think about what reliably makes you feel good about yourself and go do that before taking photos. Maybe it's a yoga class or writing in your journal. Maybe it's listening to your favorite podcast or reading the newspaper. Maybe it's sitting with a glass of wine or putting on Beethoven and turning the volume to ten. Whatever it is that makes you feel good about who you are, do that.

I have a friend who always listened to hair metal bands when she cleaned the house. Another friend bakes to get into her groove. Personally, I like to go for a run or do a quick vinyasa class to feel like I'm in the zone. Do what you do, and then capture yourself while you've still got the glow!

A Stylist's Guide to a Successful Photo Shoot

By now, you've done the thing that makes you feel like a rock star. Or at least you're feeling good about yourself. Now's the time to focus on the pictures themselves.

For most of us, having photos taken of ourselves lies somewhere between a bad day at work and having needles poked under our fingernails. But this is not the first time you've done it. You have had a yearbook photo, a DMV photo, a wedding portrait, or a passport photo taken, right? Maybe all of the above. We've all been through these moments, most likely with bad lighting and no second chances. This is going to be way easier than that! You don't have to use any of these photos. You can delete every single one of them afterward if you choose. There is no pressure to capture the most perfect image of yourself in one take.

I usually have my clients start by showing me their favorite photo of themselves. And no, it doesn't count if it's one from fifteen years ago before wrinkles, stress, divorce, and life had a say. I then have them explain to me what they like about how they look in the photo. And, most important, I ask them how the photo makes them feel when they look at it. Maybe it's the color they're wearing or their favorite piece of clothing. Maybe it's that they like the way their hair is not styled but still looks great or that they have exactly the right amount of makeup on. Maybe it's the expression on their face or the way the sunlight is hitting their hair. We want to re-create whatever it is in that favorite photo that makes them like it and feel authentically themselves.

It's worth noting that you can use this favorite photo, but it has to be within the last eighteen months, two years max. And that's only if, when all your photos are side by side, including one taken last week, you look the same in each. I can't tell you how many profiles I've seen where there is a visible span of thirteen years between all the photos. People do notice these gaps, and it will almost always be a swipe-left scenario.

First Challenge: What to Wear

Be sure not to wear your FDU (for more about the first-date uniform, see chapter 2) lest they think it's the only good outfit you own. That wouldn't be the end of the world, but you'd rather have more in your repertoire than that. Pants coupled with a silky button-down to show just enough cleavage works great. A cut-low-in-the-back dress as you look over your shoulder is a good idea for you back-loving people. Try a short skirt worn walking down the stairs if you've got legs. Personally, I like my shoulders and my legs. So, I included a shot in my profile in a short dress taken by a friend while walking down a set of stairs at an event. But I would not show pics of *both* my assets in my profile. I would save my sexy top for the first date.

As for your photos, whatever makes you feel most confident is what you should wear. If having heels on makes you feel sexier, even if it's a headshot, then by all means, wear them. Your confidence will show in your posture and your attitude.

As for choosing clothes to wear in your profile photos, they should be unfussy and uncomplicated. Even if you're a fashionista type, most men (and many women) won't understand if it's too crazy and complicated. Stay away from busy patterns and loud prints as they will just distract from *you*.

I had one young woman client who was a fashion blogger and had loads of photos of herself. They were all in very complicated fashion-forward outfits. Additionally, she was looking to the side or down in a lot of them (à la the influencer photo), so you couldn't get a good look at her face. She understood exactly what I meant when I pointed it out. It just took a second set of eyes.

When figuring out what to wear for your profile photos, think of creating a full picture of yourself. For example, a couple of casual outfits, a dressier one, possibly an activewear outfit if you're into fitness or hiking or biking, and maybe even a swimsuit shot if you are a beach person and that doesn't terrify you. Remember, you're creating a story about yourself through these six (or more) photos.

Don't worry too much about accessories and jewelry in your profile photos other than for your headshot/ main photo. The other photos won't be close enough to even notice something like earrings. When in doubt, err on the side of minimal. If you wear glasses, make sure you wear them in at least a few of your photos. And if you wear glasses all the time, you should wear them in every photo.

For the men reading this, or if you'd like to pass this on to your single guy friends, I have an important recommendation for your profile photos: if you're bald, show that you're bald! You need to own that and advertise it. Hiding it only makes it seem like something you're ashamed of. And if you think being bald is a turnoff, I have five words for you: Jamie Foxx and Ed Harris.

Hair and Makeup: How to Look Like You're Not Trying Too Hard

You can never go wrong with the real you. Get over the fact that that is the worst cliché of all time and consider how very true it is. What I mean is, if you only get a blowout on special occasions, don't have a blowout in all of your photos. If you almost always wear your hair up, wear it up in at least a couple of shots. Keep in mind, everyone's hair looks best when it's shiny. Get a good, deep conditioning mask to apply the day of your photo shoot. Or if body and volume are your challenges, then blow your hair upside down for three minutes before your shoot.

Ask Alyssa

Q: I love my gray hair, but I'm worried it will age me in my photos. Should I consider coloring it for my profile pics?

A: Don't color it for the photos unless you intend to keep doing so while you're dating. You should always look like the photos that you have on your profile.

As for makeup, wear what you would normally wear but add about 20 percent more than you would in real life. There's a reason people wear a lot of makeup for film and photos. It definitely shows you off better that way. Don't be afraid to go a little more glam than you normally would. I'm all for presenting the best version of yourself, as long as you're still recognizable. Again, do make sure you're representing the other sides of you as well.

I asked some beauty industry experts for tips that work on everyone, no matter your skin type, body type, hair type, or personality type. And, yes, such tips actually exist. I also asked for tips that don't cost a lot of money. Here's what they came up with:

1. *Curl your eyelashes before using mascara.* It's what makeup artists call a no-brainer because

it makes everyone look more awake. If you're like me and lazy and hardly ever take the time to do this unless it's for a special occasion, this is for you. Looking good for your profile pics *is* a special occasion! If you need a tutorial, there are a million how-tos on YouTube.

2. *Line the* **inside** *of your upper and lower eyelid with brown or black pencil liner.* You want to go between the eyeball and the lashes on a place makeup artists call the waterline. Make sure the pencil is super soft and super sharp. If you get queasy, muscle through. It's worth it.

3. *Pinch your cheeks.* See that color? The color of your cheeks when they're flushed is the color you are trying to approximate with a gel or cream blush. Dab the blush closer to your nose than you think—it's a common myth that it should be along your cheekbones—and rub it in until it almost disappears. When you pinch your cheeks again there should be no discernible difference between your skin and the blush.

4. *Exfoliate your lips with a soft, dry toothbrush.* This is an old makeup-artist trick to make the lips soft and plump and sexy. Follow it with a lightly tinted lip gloss or Vaseline. This isn't a vampy, full-color moment. Merely a sweet, glossy, soft mouth.

Ultimately, beauty is about looking healthy, so whatever way you can achieve this, that's what looks good to others.

Get the Light Right

The golden hour, roughly an hour after the sun rises and then the hour before the sun sets, is considered the magical time of day for photography due to the amazing color and quality of the light. Obviously, it's not imperative that you take your profile photos during these times, but you will find the light to be very flattering if you do.

As a beginner, it's always easier to take your photos outside. If you need or want to do indoor shots, use window light for the best light. And, of course, if you're using natural light, it should be directed on your face. You can even set your phone up on the windowsill on a timer and face the window. Typically, using the flash isn't as flattering, but play around with it.

To give you the best tips, I asked one of the industry's top professionals, New York City fashion and portrait photographer Andrew Day, for a few lighting secrets.

Secrets for Capturing Your Selfie in the Best Light

- First, find the best location for light in your home, preferably with the same type of light. For example, most house lights are very yellow. But office lights and bathroom lights can be blue or a mixture. So, if you are using more than one light, make sure they are giving off a similar color.

- When you're taking photos inside, use indirect light whenever possible. For example, point your lamp at the wall or bounce the light off the ceiling at an angle. Avoid lighting that is directly overhead.

- When you're taking photos outside, find a shaded side of the house or building. Don't worry if it's a cloudy day. People always complain about overcast days when we shoot, but photographers love it. It's easier to warm up the tone on the photograph and still get all the details you want without being blasted by light or harsh shadows.

- If you want to get a little technical, put something white underneath your face. It can be a hand towel or a piece of printer paper from your home office, anything bright white. This will help fill in shadows under your eyes and give a subtle glow.

What's Behind You?

This is an extremely common mistake in people's photos, whether for dating or social media. Your hair is perfectly blowing in the wind, you're wearing exactly the right thing, with a sparkle in your eye ... and your bright-blue trash can is behind you with garbage spilling out of it in the background. Do check your background. Ideally, it should be something simple or that fades away. When all else fails, a plain white wall will work. Even better would be a white brick wall to give it some texture. Trees in the background work well, as does a beach or water scene. If you're more confident with photography, you can use a cool mural or a more scenic view. Be sure you mix it up—you don't want to have the same background in every photo.

I've seen countless photos with something behind the person in the distance that looks like it's sticking out from the top of the person's head. I've seen even more with a messy kitchen or bedroom in the background. Double-check all around you before taking a photo. Or when you're selecting from your existing photos, zoom in to make sure there are no surprises.

Time to Shoot

There are a few types of selfies—the selfie where you hold
your arm out and flip the camera to face you, the selfie
where you shoot your reflection in the mirror, and the selfie where you put it on a timer. The word "selfie" has become a broad term, but of course it's officially a selfie if it
was taken by . . . yourself. In my opinion, and after working
with many different clients, people aren't all that interested in a profile that consists of only the arm-held-out
selfie photos. It starts to enter Kardashian territory if
there are more than a couple of those. You need to have a
varied mix. Sometimes it's worthwhile to go to the effort
of making a selfie photo look like it was taken by someone
else, such as setting a timer. Because, let's face it, you are
only going to get your best friend to take your photo so
many times.

To many of us, even the word "selfie" conjures up images of narcissistic and self-focused celebrities (see *Kardashian* above). To some, it's a way to make a living (the
influencer). And for some, it's a way to get a date (you and
me). Social media has made "selfie" a household word, but
it doesn't have to mean anything other than expressing
yourself in order for people to see a certain side of you.
And just know going into this practice session, you will
probably look through the first dozen tries and only think
of Blue Steel from the movie *Zoolander*.

The first few times I took a selfie, I confess, I felt ridiculous. But as with pretty much anything, you get used to it with repetition. Selfies aren't simply something you go out and do, they are something you have to practice. I realized that pretty quickly after my first few tries, and boy, did I have my work cut out for me.

I would come home from a date or going out with my friends, when my hair was not just thrown into a bun and I had mascara on, and go for it. I probably deleted the first seven hundred selfies. In the first several hundred, I was either staring intently or, worse, blankly at my own reflection, which definitely does not work. The next several hundred were of me half blinking, which is never a flattering shot.

I looked back at all the photos and laughed at my attempts at a fake smile or a trying-to-be-sexy look. I felt so old suddenly. I had to experiment with facial expressions and positions and head tilts. It was embarrassing and at times humiliating, and I kept thinking that if anyone were spying on me and watching me in my apartment late at night (okay, that would be even more creepy and weird than me taking selfies), they would think of me as self-obsessed and vain.

At the time, I was working with a lot of people much younger than I was. One of the twenty-something hairstylists who was on set with me had watched me standing on the set, in between shots, with my arm outstretched, attempting some selfies. I'd tried to be covert about it, but she caught me red-handed, trying to look cute, staring at my own reflection. She came over and immediately put me at ease because, at her age, everyone does this.

She gave me a few pointers: face directly into the beauty light (yes, that's what that professional light is called) with my arm raised slightly, and then make sure I'm feeling something—happiness, sexiness, anything but vacant eyes. I was forever grateful, and after exchanging some of our online dating woes, we became friends.

I realized over time that I had a benevolent army of women around me—at work, at home, in my life—who wanted me to succeed. They wanted me out of my marriage, they wanted me out of a bad situation, and they wanted me to find my happiness. It was a supportive, invisible force that buoyed me, whether or not I even knew they were there. Whatever they could do to help, no matter what age they were, whether they had been married themselves or not, the women around me lifted me up in a way I had never experienced before. It's an incredibly empowering force knowing that there is a support network rooting for you in your corner, no matter what. And by the way, once you find that uplifting network, taking a selfie is way easier.

I eventually got the hang of the selfie, and some of them made it onto my profile or even into a late-night text exchange with a new Tinder match. The best time to practice the selfie is when you know you are looking good. We all get this feeling at least once in a while. And I hope, since you've been single, you have treated yourself to that new pair of shoes that make you feel sexy or some new highlights that make you feel five years younger. So, it's time to put those things to use and practice that selfie.

The Non-selfie

When you can convince a good friend to take some photos for your profile, make sure she knows that you don't mean simply snapping five shots of you and then moving on to her latest work drama she wants to share. You mean you want a mini photo shoot. You need her to take a hundred shots (yes, actually) of the same outfit from a bunch of different angles. Promise a bottle of wine or treat her to dinner in exchange, to show her that this is a real favor and you're serious about it.

When you think about posing, forget about your "good side." Unless you're Julia Roberts and have had approximately one million photo shoots, most of us don't know our good side. Experiment. Try a few new head tilts or smiles that you haven't tried before. You would be surprised at how many times I've worked with clients taking photos, and they are shocked that an angle they didn't think would work is their best yet.

Last but not least, if you've asked a few friends and either they say no or you try it and neither of you feels comfortable and you hate all of the photos, it's time to consider hiring a professional photographer.

I remember the first time I asked one of my best friends (okay, fine, it was Jocelyn again), who was married and not online dating, to come over to take some shots of me in and around my apartment. I felt so self-conscious even asking. She made it easy on me and even pretended to be excited. When she came over that day, I was nervous. I had spent my whole adult life around photographers—have I mentioned my ex-husband was a photographer? You would think that would make me feel more comfortable in front of the camera. Well, you would be wrong. It took a lot of those mini photo shoots to get more and more relaxed.

A gentle reminder: if you do have a successful photo session, whether that's a round of selfies one night or a shoot with a friend, you can only use one photo per outfit. You don't want to have a profile where you look like you had a photo session, and you're wearing the same exact thing in each photo. So, line up a few different outfits for the shoot and plan enough time to include wardrobe changes.

Ask Alyssa

Q: I keep taking selfies and having friends snap photos when we're together, but I'm so unphotogenic. I hate all of them!

A: Everyone feels this way. Pretty much no one I know loves photos of themselves. Most people who are "naturally photogenic" are simply people who are used to having photos taken and know their best ways to smile and tilt their head, which means they have practiced. So, once again, practice makes perfect.

To Be or Not to Be (Too) Sexy: How Much Sex Appeal Is the Right Amount?

Some women come to me and say these exact words: "My best friend/mom/therapist/guy friend told me I need to look sexy in all my profile photos. So, let's do this." My response is always, "Do you want to just have sex?" If the answer is yes, then by all means, yes, let's sex you up for every picture. Zero judgment. But, if you're looking for more than a hookup, you need to have an assortment of photos in varying degrees of sexiness.

As my client Allison learned the hard way, you need to have sex appeal without screaming SEX. If you have six photos on your profile (you should have at least that), have one or two that are sexy or alluding to sexy. For example, if you're super proud of your back, then show a photo in a backless dress. But make sure it's only one. If you are a cleavage girl, go for that with one of the sexier pics. Love your legs? Then by all means, show them off. And it doesn't have to be something so overt. You can show a sliver of your ankles and that can be sexy. But please don't show all of these things. Pick one area of skin to show off. Leave a little to the imagination, and add a smile so that you don't look, as the kids say these days, "thirsty."

The sexy thing, however, is a matter of interpretation. What a sexy photo is to some people would be pornographic to others. And what is sexy to one person would feel like a LinkedIn photo to yet another person. Think about what is sexy to you personally. Think about what makes you feel sexy. Maybe it's dancing to a few of the sexiest songs you know before your photo. Or maybe putting on some winged eyeliner or having a coy smile can feel sexy to you. In other words, it doesn't have to be showing skin to be a "sexy" photo. Warning to some of you: Sometimes when people try to do a sexy face, it instead looks mad or unhappy. Make sure you practice in the mirror and check in with yourself that you're getting the right look across.

A Smile Is Inviting

You don't have to have an ear-to-ear grin in every photo, but at least a few of the photos need to be smiley ones. And when you're not grinning, make sure you're smiling with your eyes—as Tyra Banks says, "smizing."

One thing I have to say after years of taking photos of people, whether they are models on a shoot or real people for their profile photos, a fake smile doesn't look fake to anyone else, specifically someone who doesn't even know you. It may feel fake and look fake to you, but trust me, it won't to other people, other than your mother who in theory won't be seeing your dating profile. Hopefully the person taking the photos can make you laugh. Or you can try the trick of thinking of something funny to get a real smile on your face.

I had a guy client who looked super tough and serious in every photo, and he wondered why he wasn't getting any matches. It was the easiest fix ever. We took a bunch of new photos in which he was smiling in each photo, and he was shocked by the difference it made.

The bottom line here is this: be approachable. If you're smiling, you seem friendly, and if you're friendly, you're approachable. People want to match with someone they think they'll feel comfortable with. Someone who is warm and friendly, not cold and aloof.

Posing and Expressions

Remember those Olan Mills photos in the eighties where you were resting your chin on your fist or you had one hand on your hip in a super-forced way? Yeah, that's the opposite of what we're going for here. But if we were all Instagram influencers and knew how to take the perfect "candid" photo, life would be pretty boring. This is another thing that takes practice. Learning what face tilt or hand position or stance works best for you personally takes many photos and tries. Remember to try lots of different poses and facial expressions whether it's a selfie or a shoot with a friend or professional. Don't give up. Look at Instagram or a magazine to get some ideas.

Here's more advice from professional fashion and portrait photographer Andrew Day. He says good posture is always key. An industry trick he suggests is to put your arms above your head and out to the side to straighten your posture and shoulders.

He also reiterates to be yourself: "Embrace whatever makes you unique, and have fun with it. Try as many angles as you can. While you are in between clicks, move your chin up a little, down a little, and to the left and right, ever so slightly each frame."

I've had a few widowed or divorced clients who, being very new to online dating, thought hiring a professional photographer was the clear way to go. They come to me after months of being online, wondering why they aren't getting a lot of messaging on Match. When I look at their photos, they are completely staged studio shots, hands on hips like Superwoman or looking over their shoulder à la Olan Mills. If you are going to hire a professional, make sure it's someone familiar with online dating or who takes online dating photos regularly. People see these staged studio shots and run for the hills.

Filters

Nowadays, people can spot a filtered photo from a mile away. I generally steer clients away from using filters. One reason is that a lot of them are just plain cheesy looking. But another issue that comes with filters is that you can start to second-guess every single photo and think it must need a filter to look good. "Should I saturate more or less?" "Should I do Rio or should I do Paris?" This is a rabbit hole you can go down and never come out of.

I had a sixty-year-old client come to me with some great photos she already had that we immediately put up on her profile. A few weeks later, she discovered the selfie and started sending them to me for my feedback. These were also great. Then she discovered the filter, and it went downhill from there. She looked blemish- and line-free, but obviously filtered. I told her to stick to her great selfie skills without the filter.

I am, however, in favor of a little light retouching. Maybe you have a pimple, maybe you had a sunburn that day, maybe you have flyaways but it's otherwise a great photo. Or maybe it's a weird angle that's making your arm look thicker than it is (99.9 percent of women have felt this way on more than one occasion). It's okay to lightly retouch. Either download an app and do it yourself if that's your thing, have a friend do it, or even hire someone to do it for you. Adjusting these minor issues does not change your overall appearance or who you are. You're simply making a good photo even better. I will say it again: the goal here is to look like the best version of yourself.

Cropping and Editing

Cropping in on a photo can make or break it. It's so easy now to crop into a photo and then, if you don't like it, simply don't save it. But don't crop out your ex. It's more obvious than you would think when people do this. Another case of bad cropping is one client who had photo after photo of him out at a party or a club. He cropped into the photos so you could only see his own face with a blurry sea of skin and un-focused arms and legs behind him (people apparently wear next to nothing at clubs). He had three of the same type of photo, all with the same expression too. It not only showed one side of his personality (a partier) at the exclusion of all others, but it gave no variation to his expression, not to mention the distraction of all the blurry bodies behind him.

On the other hand, an example of good cropping is when you have a photo but maybe you aren't sucking in your gut, your fly is down, or you have an outdated style of jeans on, and you crop to make it a chest-up shot. Do be sure, though, that it's high enough resolution so that it's not grainy when it's cropped.

Editing a photo to make it brighter or more contrasted can also vastly improve a so-so photo. There are many editing apps you can download now to do this yourself. One editor of a very popular beauty magazine told me to make the photos I take 10 percent darker—this subtle difference makes your skin look clearer. Think about it: everyone looks better by candlelight.

Here's some advice from my friend and professional fashion, portrait, and lifestyle photographer Marsha Bernstein: "Don't be afraid of those photo edit functions (not to be confused with filters) on your phone. If you feel like your face looks too blue or orange, slide the temperature slider up or down to make you look more like yourself. A touch too dark? Increase the exposure or brightness. Experiment and make sure the final result feels natural and looks flattering."

You may even want to try one of your favorite photos in black and white. As long as it's not more than one and it's of you, I say throw one in to see if it sticks. See how people respond to it.

Videos on Apps

A couple of the dating apps offer this feature. The videos can only be a few seconds long, so you have to be quick and creative about it. Many of my clients are too nervous to add this to their profile. They feel too much pressure to make something interesting while also being cool and sexy, but not too sexy. People spend a ridiculous amount of time on these videos. My advice if you do want to add one: look through the videos you already have on your phone. Maybe one with friends that feels less forced and more natural would be a good choice. If there's no appropriate video in your archives and you still want to do a video, create it. Then, make sure you run it by friends for a reality check before you upload it onto a dating app.

As I mentioned earlier and want to reiterate here, if you have photos that are older than a year and a half or two years max, they are disqualified. How would you feel if you showed up and the person was much older than in his or her photos? You would feel duped. Even though that person, or you, may not be doing it to trick anyone, one can't help but feel misled.

I have a client who, no matter how many times I told her she had to update her photos—I even offered to do it for her with no additional cost—insisted on using photos that were more than five years old. She consistently never got asked out for a second date. Not because she was unfriendly or unattractive, but, in my opinion, because every date showed up expecting one thing but got something else, and then left feeling resentful or, even worse, catfished.

Photo-Bio Synergy

Make sure your photos match your bio. There has to be synergy between how you're describing yourself and what you show in your photos. For example, you say you're shy but you're partying in every shot. I have a young client who wanted to be taken more seriously and meet a long-term partner. She was super sweet with a good head on her shoulders. However, her profile was six photos of her with at least two friends, if not five, out at either a bar or club in every single shot. She was all but saying to people, "I just want to party." Replacing a lot of her photos with some daytime shots and shots of her alone sent a different message.

Is It You?

Do your profile pics represent you? Do they align with who you say you are? Take a step back and view your photos as someone else would. Or better yet, ask a friend or two to look at them and give you honest feedback. The photos are, at the end of the day, the most important part of your profile to attract the right match. They're what people look at first and what grabs them or not. Once people see a photo they like, *then* they read the bio to find out more.

Not enough women—or men—ask for help when it comes to their dating profile. Women tend to be better at asking for help than most men, for sure, but we could still improve. Even if, like me, you don't have many unmarried friends, you should at least ask the opinion of your married ones. They know you, know what you're looking for, and what you should be putting out there to the online world. So, put your pride aside and ask for advice and/or help with a photo shoot.

I was so uplifted by the support of my tribe of women who were there for me during my divorce, dating, and being a single mom. By the end of this process, I had more than just photos of myself—I had explored myself in a new way. I'd come closer to the essence of who I am. Embarrassing asks of selfie lessons and mini photo sessions are a distant memory that no one but me thought about for even a second. It made me realize how strong my friendships are. And that people want to help—you only have to ask. Whatever community you have, there is a sisterhood that is waiting for you. You simply have to look for it. You'll be rewarded greatly. I promise. Maybe a selfie is "all you," but it's the best representation of you when you're feeling loved and supported by your friends.

Style Your Selfie Cheat Sheet

- As you get better at taking selfies and having your photo taken, keep switching out your profile pics with the better, updated ones.
- Plan out the six shots you need for your profile: headshot, active shot, social shot, full-body shot, the just-sexy-enough shot, and dealer's choice.
- Keep photos recent. Don't use any photos that are older than a year and a half, two years maximum.
- Before a photo shoot, pump yourself up with music, wine, yoga, a run, whatever gets you in the zone and glowing.
- Wear an outfit that's not your FDU (first-date uniform), and that shows a little skin but leaves something to the imagination and makes you feel confident.

- Wear your hair as you usually wear it for most of your pictures and wear the same kind of makeup but about 20 percent more.

- Take your photos in natural light—outdoor light is easiest for beginners. If you're inside, try light from a window or indirect light rather than direct light.

- Use a simple background or one that fades away, and be sure to check that there's nothing in the background that you wouldn't want in the picture.

- Smile, even if you're faking it, for at least a few of the photos, if not more.

- Experiment and have fun with poses and expressions. While you're posing, be feeling something—happiness, sexiness, and so on—to avoid vacant eyes.

- Ditch filters, but do use cropping and light retouching carefully when necessary.

- Make sure it's you—that your photo matches who you say you are in your bio, and that it feels and looks like the real you.

- Get help from friends—their support can make all the difference.

5

Style Your Swiping

Swipe #1

Now, here's where we get real. Online dating goes from a what-if to—let's be honest—something that can consume a significant part of your waking hours. It's scary, exciting, and at first you might be so buzzed by the experience that, like me, you'll have a hard time putting your phone down. You might have a slow start or you might have a super-fast takeoff with lots of matches. Either way, you will have ups and downs along the way with plenty of chances to adjust your bio, pics, and preferences. Enjoy those first thrilling weeks, but keep your view for the long haul. It took me more than two years of swiping, messaging, texting, talking, and IRL (in real life) dating, but I did finally swipe on the right man.

So, how did I make it through years of swipes? It all started with an app.

Which App Is Right for Me?

When you first consider going online to date, it probably overwhelms you to think of all the apps out there. I'll give you the lowdown on the main ones here so you can figure out the best place for you to start.

There are also plenty of apps for people looking for more specialized pools of users, such as those geared toward LGBTQIA, Christians, Jews, people living in rural areas, people who are really into books, and the list goes on. Search online for almost any category you can think of, and you'll probably find a dating app for it, but I really like the wider net you get on the more popular apps I've focused on.

If you want immediate gratification, head to **Tinder** for sure. And not necessarily the kind of gratification that involves sex. I mean, sure, sex, too, as this can and does happen. But also I'm also talking about the ego-lifting gratification of getting matches. My female clients who are unsure of themselves or the process need to be shown that it does "work." In my office, I've helped them upload a few photos and a brief bio. I've sat there and watched women match with people within seconds of swiping. It's an instant ego boost. Tinder has more people on the app than any other, no matter what city you're in. And, of course, Tinder has a soft spot in my heart because it's where I started and ended online dating. It's how I met my partner.

Bumble is also a swiping app. It's similar to Tinder except that once you match with a potential date, the woman (in hetero dynamics) is responsible for reaching out first or the match expires in twenty-four hours. This setup is good for women who are nervous about being on an app where men can reach out first. It makes them feel more in control. I personally didn't like the pressure of having to make the first move, but many women do. And because of this, a lot of men prefer it too.

Match is the more serious of the apps, mainly because you have to pay for it. So, naturally it attracts people who are really wanting to meet someone. I would say, for people in metropolitan areas, it generally attracts people over the age of forty-five, but if you're in a suburb or more rural area, it's more of an all-ages app.

For any of my clients under fifty, **Hinge** is the app of the moment that I recommend. There is no bio—instead they have you choose questions to answer creatively that divulge things about you.

OkCupid is great if you want to know, before you meet, if your potential date likes to be whipped during sex. I'm only half kidding here. OkCupid has a very lengthy questionnaire, and it encourages users to answer as many questions as possible. So, in theory, by answering these very personal questions, which other people can view, you are offered potential matches who are like-minded. I met one person on OkCupid whom I dated for several months, and we joked that there are some things you just don't need to know about a person before you have even met, never mind had sex. That being said, a lot of people like this app.

If you're a creative (or happen to be a model or a celebrity), then you can "apply" to the now-exclusive app **Raya**. It was fairly new when I was on it in 2016 so it has a lot more people now. I referred to it as "window shopping," because there were a lot of interesting and good-looking people on there, but hardly anyone messaged after matching. I only went out with one person from this app. We happen to still be friends, so I guess it worked out in that respect. I have since heard from other women that not much has changed since I was on it. It's also an app where you curate your profile and even add music and videos to it.

Another app that many people like because of the small pool of people is **The League**. It is geared toward professionals and college grads. It's not as active as some of the other apps, because it's not a swiping app. The app selects certain people to show you each day. But some people like not having so many people to sort through and message with.

I recommend trying out several apps at once. After even a few days, you'll get a better idea of what app feels the best. The functionality and the user interface are all slightly different. Find the one that fits you.

For continually updated information on all of the dating apps, go to *stylemyprofile.com*.

Don't Style Your Soul Mate

So, you're starting to get some matches. Now is the time to keep an open mind rather than looking at every match and finding something wrong with it.

"He's not my type." "Nice, but not for me." "Cute, but I don't see it." "Not feeling it." These are all versions of the same self-defeating, limiting plotline, and I've heard it a million times from my clients over the years. Usually they say it after they've looked at a picture. The idea of someone being someone else's "type" is insane. We're not auto parts that need to fit properly into a combustible engine.

My friend Nina says again and again, "He's too old." Meanwhile, he is the same age she is. Female daters are as guilty as their male counterparts of wanting to date younger people. So, you know where that leaves everyone? Single. Everyone feels younger than they are. Everyone feels like they look younger than they are. We have to stop perpetuating this model of dating.

Keep an open mind and don't narrow your age parameters. A lot of people may look "old" to you in a photo, but when you meet in person, it's a different story altogether. It takes an IRL date to get a real feel for someone's age. And by this I don't mean the number, I mean vitality and spirit.

Take Emily. She doesn't want to date someone "too old," so she only goes for guys her age or younger. But she keeps heading into her first dates assuming these younger guys won't ask her out again anyway. She had a couple of bad experiences in the beginning of her postdivorce online dating that really stuck with her. So, even a couple of years later, she sabotages every date with a defeatist attitude about herself and dating. She's styling her future date as someone who automatically doesn't like her.

Her therapist finally said to her, "What if you go into each date with the attitude of 'Will *I* like *him*?' instead of the other way around?" And just like that, everything changed. Not only that, but the guy she ended up dating long term was older than the guys she had been going for previously. She was shocked at how into him she was. They totally clicked.

It's Dating 101. Restrictions and prejudgments can sabotage any relationship before you're even out of the gate.

People are multidimensional. We're all shades of gray. We're all shades of all colors. If you've always been into only tall guys, date a guy your own height. If you've always been into business types, go out with a teacher. There are many ways to expand your horizons. At minimum, you'll learn something new about yourself.

If you go into online dating thinking your new partner has to look this way and dress that way and have this job and that lifestyle, you will continue to be disappointed.

Obviously, there will be things you don't want to concede on, like destructive behaviors, drug use, and so on. My advice is to get out there and date—in real life, in person, and with all different types of people. Experiment by going out with someone who is decidedly not your type.

While working in the magazine world for many years, I was assigned to edit fashion stories like "10 Things You Should Get Your Guy to Wear" and similar fixer-upper articles. The truth is, none of that is going to stick. People are who they are.

Take my friend Charlie, who fell in love with a creative writer. For years, she kept buying him dress shirts, cuff links, and ties, thinking that even though he wasn't a banker, she could dress him like one. He got the message loud and clear . . . and rejected it. He loved his ripped jeans and T-shirts and broken-in, old New Balance sneakers. Charlie was not going to be styled by her, because he already had a style he liked just fine.

Sure, you can nudge your boyfriend or girlfriend to take something out of rotation, and he or she might even do it. But the best style is the one that is the most authentic. When people are truly in love and right for each other, they don't try to change or style each other. You can style yourself and you can help style your friends *if* they ask for help, but you can't style your partner—unless, of course, your partner actually wants to be styled. Even then, you have to tread lightly. Really lightly. In fact, bad idea. Don't do it.

A Cautionary Tale

You should also think of the whole "styling your soul mate" thing in reverse. You don't want to be the person who is so eager to find a mate that you're willing to become whatever your mate wants. We all know this logically. But sometimes it can happen without us knowing it. I have an old friend, Roger, who so wanted to meet the girl of his dreams that every time he dated someone new, he would change himself to some degree (sometimes a larger degree than others). He wanted to be made into whatever the person he was dating wanted. He was the sophisticated traveler boyfriend, then he was the art-lover boyfriend, then he was handy, fix-anything boyfriend, then he was country club boyfriend.

The women he dated didn't see it, because he was so good at becoming whatever it was they were attracted to. He wasn't being malicious or manipulative; he simply wanted to please whomever he was with and wanted them to like him. You don't want to be that person. And you want to find a partner who is not that person. Be true to who you are, and don't change for someone just because you want a partner.

Texting, Emojis, and Acronyms: Communicating Shouldn't Be This Hard

I had a few unpleasant experiences right off the bat. There were moments I thought I wasn't cut out for online dating and communicating via app and text. But I kept at it. I realized that there was a dance to it all: When to reach out first, when to respond, when to ask someone out, when to be flirty. And when things got too sexty, how to dial it back.

I was usually on two or three apps at a time—it was somewhere between a curiosity and a part-time job. There were many nights after my kids went to bed that I would be messaging with people well into the wee hours. My friends at work laughed at me because whenever I didn't have my kids, which—with 50 percent custody—was a lot, I was going out on a date right after work. One friend called it my new hobby. It wasn't only about finding a love connection. I found it fun and fascinating to meet new people and hear their personal stories. I've said it to friends again and again—I learned so much about myself during those years of first and second dates and telling and retelling my own story. I also regained even more confidence discovering my true self and finding that I was actually an interesting person.

When it comes to communicating with matches, you can choose to only communicate on the apps themselves. All the apps have a way to text without giving anyone your number. This provides a nice barrier for you to practice your matching and communication before you commit to giving out more personal information or your number for texting.

With some of the apps, you need to match with the person before you can reach out—Tinder and Bumble, for example—and for others, you can reach out to anyone—like Match and OkCupid. And then there's Hinge, where you can comment on someone's photo before matching with him or her. Once you have a few messages and then texts back and forth and establish a connection, it can be fun to start a flirty banter to get a better feel for one another. This flirtation sometimes happens even before your first date, depending on the person and the connection you have over text. Or it develops once you've already met in person and like each other.

Flirting over text can quickly turn to sexting, so if you're not ready for that—and no judgment if you are!—it's good to have a few responses up your sleeve to dial it back without putting an end to the texting. I sometimes fell back on making a joke out of it and calling the person on moving too fast, which usually worked well. I'd respond with something like, "Whoa, there!" An emoji like ✖ or 🙈 can also help you say "no" or "slow down" in a nonaggressive way. If I really wanted to get the point across, I would be direct: "I prefer to meet in person before going there."

Then there's the question of how quickly to respond to a text—how to appear interested but not desperate. Again, this is something that you have to get a feel for. With some people, it's fine with them if you do not respond for a day. With others, not so much. After my boyfriend and I became an official couple, he confessed that many times while dating early on he'd thought I wasn't interested and he should move on. He said that I wasn't very responsive, and it was extremely frustrating. I was surprised to hear this as I felt like a pretty texty person. But he'd had other dates who had been more so, and he thought it was a sign that I was only half in. So, like anything else, it's a balance and something you'll eventually get into a groove with what works best for you.

Ask Alyssa

Q: I've been on a dating app for about four weeks now. I haven't swiped on anyone yet. Looking at their pics and bios, I don't "feel it." Am I being too picky? Should I choose someone who seems normal just to try it out? Maybe I'm putting too much pressure on the process to find the "perfect" guy. At the same time, I don't want to waste my time or the other person's. Can you help me make my first swipe?

A: As I've said many times about online dating: rip the Band-Aid off! The more you do it, the easier it will be. Swiping on someone doesn't mean you're going on a date with them. So, start with swiping then move to messaging. Baby steps.

What Should I Say to Start a Conversation with Someone?

This is the million-dollar question. People want a magic text to which every person with whom you match will respond to. I wish it were that simple. If it were, I really would be a billionaire. However, after much experience myself and with my clients, I have come up with some things to think about to get your message read and replied to:

1. **Focus on quality, not quantity.** Don't message with too many people at once. Message with just a few so you can focus on making good conversation with those few.

2. **Compliment common interests and personality, not looks.** People want to know that you're reaching out for more than just how they look. That can come later.

3. **Stake out common ground, be positive, and focus on the person's unique qualities.**

4. **Ask questions. And keep asking!** This is a great way to get a conversation going—and keep it going—and to learn about someone.

5. **Keep it short and simple.** Don't get into long texts right away. You don't need to go into detail when telling a story or something about yourself. Not until you've messaged for a while.

6. **Reread what you wrote before you hit send.** Make sure your message makes sense and check for spelling, grammar, and typos.

On the Hinge app, conversations start with a prompt.

Best season of Game of Thrones: GO!

Is it heretical to say Season 8, since that's the only one I've seen?

You've gotta be kidding. You've really only seen Season 8?

Shockingly yes! I had my friends give me a 30-minute crash course before starting, and then I spent each episode trying to swallow many, many additional questions

I'm so sorry you've been deprived of the cinematic masterpiece that is seasons 1-7. But as someone who has a strict no talking during movies policy, I admire your restraint! Hope it wasn't too confusing ultimately

I see you're into hiking, which is a much more admirable hobby than watching GoT. Any good hikes recently?

Yes, in fact! I just did Mt. Mansfield, the tallest peak in Vermont. Ate my weight in ice cream when I finished.

Do you hike?

I do! Here's what I think we should do. Date 1, ice cream. Date 2, climb a mountain. Date 3, watch all of GoT seasons 1-7 in one sitting. Sound good?

I'm always down for ice cream. Maybe a drink as well. How does next week look?

Communicating and Then Some . . .

When you go from communicating on an app to exchanging numbers and texting, you're letting this person into your life a little bit. This can be exciting but also weird, especially when you're new to online dating. I occasionally made this transition too quickly, but not to the point that it was ever a big deal. In two and a half years, I only had to block someone from texting my number once. The guy was about ten years younger than I was. Our first date was pretty average, although he was maybe a little more forward than some. We agreed to go out a second time. He had my number, and the day before our date, he texted me saying he'd gotten some Molly and thought it would be fun to do this together. On our *second date*. I declined, saying my drug-experimenting days were over, and I had two daughters to think of. He went on a text rant about how I was using my kids as an excuse to not get close to people.

I didn't even reply. Then he kept texting and even tried calling me. I blocked him and luckily never heard from him again. To be honest, in addition to blocking his number, I have even blocked out his name.

I recommend waiting until there is some kind of connection, at the very least, before giving out your cell number. Some people even wait until after they've met in person.

Texting can be misread even with someone you know very well, never mind someone you've never met. This is where emojis come in handy. It used to be something for the kids and early millennials. But it's now become a language that even my oldest clients use for messaging. Punctuating with an emoji can make or break a text. Some feel that people have become reliant on emojis and they are a bit of a crutch, but I disagree. Using emojis is a way to show that a message that could be interpreted as arrogant or complaining or negative was actually meant to be sarcastic or funny. Of course, don't go overboard with emoji use. Most often, less is more.

There are now even widely accepted emoji meanings that originated as something seemingly unrelated (eggplant or peach, anyone?). I dated some people who spoke the language of emojis, and some who didn't. Sometimes you have to ask what something means and that's okay. That's also what friends and Urban Dictionary are for.

Sometimes miscommunication will occur. I had a client, Rebecca, who was reluctant to date after her divorce. She came to me when she finally decided she was ready to get online. I set her up on an app, and she was swiping and messaging immediately. She discovered a new online dating "code" that I had heard about but hadn't mentioned to her. This was knowledge she probably wished she could have done without.

She matched with a guy she thought was very good-looking. She couldn't figure out why he showed only parts of his face and body in his (only two) photos. They texted back and forth. Rebecca felt like his messages were a little forward, but she was attracted to him and eager to date. They met for drinks, and when Rebecca arrived, her date handed her a wrapped present. She was hesitant, but also curious. She opened the box. Inside was a pair of leather handcuffs!

Seeing the shocked look on her face, he explained that he was into BDSM (bondage/discipline, domination/submission), and he was confused about why she didn't know that from his profile. Apparently, a sign for being into BDSM can be not showing your whole face and body in your profile pics. Who knew?

So, the lesson here is this: There will be some mixed messages. There will be a learning curve. Not everyone you meet in person will be a match, even if you had a good rapport messaging back and forth. Be up front, ask questions, and don't ever feel pressured to take the conversation or the relationship places you're not ready or interested to go.

Here are some of the abbreviations, acronyms, and terms used in texting that the younger generations have as part of their vernacular but we middle-aged and older folk need some help with. The longer someone has been online, the more they are used to this kind of texting.

Texting Cheat Sheet

BDSM: Thanks to *Fifty Shades of Grey*, we're all pretty familiar with Bondage/Discipline, Domination/Submission. *No, you do not have to be into this to do online dating! But if you are, you will find a lot of like-minded people.*

D&D free, D/D free, D/D, or DD: Drug- and Disease-Free. *This is obviously a good thing, but it may be worth asking yourself why they're even mentioning it.*

DTE: Down to Earth. *And yet somehow using the acronym sort of cancels it out.*

Exing: Unable to get over an ex. *Be thankful for the red flag and swipe on.*

F2F: Face-to-Face. *Good to know they are up for meeting in person and not just texting.*

FWB: Friends with Benefits. *I think we've all heard of this, thanks to the movie.*

IRL: In Real Life. *As in an actual face-to-face date.*

LDR: Long-Distance Relationship. *This is something to consider, whether you're interested in this or not. I personally didn't think I would be, but then was fine when it happened.*

LGBTQIA: Lesbian, Gay, Bisexual, Transgender, Queer, Intersex, and Ally. *It's always good to keep track of what terminology is being used.*

LS: Legally Separated or Light Smoker. *Very good to know which one they're talking about.*

LTR: Long-Term Relationship. *This would be the opposite of a "hookup."*

MBA: Married but Available. *Save yourself. Run!*

NBM: Never Been Married. *Sometimes this is good to know.*

ND or N/D: Nondrinker, No Drinking, or No Drugs. *Possibly all of the above.*

NSA: No Strings Attached. *Another way to say FWB or "hookup."*

Pan: Pansexual, meaning interested in all sexes, genders, and gender identities. *Again, good to know beforehand.*

Poly: Polyamorous, meaning people interested in intimate relationships with more than one person. *Some consider this is a nicer way of saying nonmonogamous. You decide.*

SO: Significant Other. *I'm assuming this would be in the "looking for" rather than the "already have" scenario.*

SOH/GSOH: Sense of Humor/Great or Good Sense of Humor. *Maybe consider whether someone who claims to have a "Great SOH" actually could.*

TG: Transgender. *Another good one to know before you meet.*

TS: Transsexual. *See TG above.*

VBD: Very Bad Date. *Would they be describing themselves with this one? If so, swipe left, please.*

W: Widowed or White. *Or possibly even the forty-third president? As acronyms go, this one is a land mine of potential confusion.*

WAA: Will Answer All. *As in "will answer any question posed." Would you really agree to this?*

Wingman: A person who helps a friend meet people. *The reference is from the 1980s hit movie* Top Gun, *which may or may not be a good thing.*

Red Flags Spanning from Pink to Burgundy: There Is a Spectrum

This is the time to talk about the messages that give you a twinge of . . . a bad feeling. Things that you would possibly leave out when telling a friend about someone you're messaging with or going out on a date with. Things that just don't sit right. If you have trouble identifying them, think of it this way: Is there anything about this person that you'd rather not focus on? Red flag. At least a pink-tinged one.

Look for people who take their profile seriously. If they have only one picture, there's a 99 percent chance that they are either not into this whole idea of online dating, they think they are too good for this, or they are married. If they don't have a bio, it is likely the same. And as I always say, if they can't take two minutes to write something, then they may also not be the person who will put any effort in.

Another thing that I'm sure you've all heard of at this point are the young guys who are looking for a cougar, or older woman. This is a thing.

Being a newbie to all of this, I remember matching with a much younger guy and actually being flattered that this twenty-four-year-old (!!) was interested in me. At the time I was forty-one. I thought that maybe he didn't see my age. Keep in mind that this was one of my first matches and also one of my first exchanges. After messaging for a little while one late afternoon, he asked if I wanted to meet him that night at an art show he was going to. Did I mention he was extremely attractive? I almost said yes, but said I was in for the evening.

The next day, I saw he'd unmatched me. When I texted Cool Single Friend asking what she thought, she was unphased. "Oh, yeah, young guys always want to meet older women." I dug a little deeper with some other single friends and found out this is for two reasons: 1) because we have either been married before and/or are past the having-kids stage, and 2) because we are much more comfortable with who we are, in our own skin, than their twenty- or thirty-something counterparts. They like that they can hang out for a while, have great sex, and not feel like we want to get married and have a family. Lesson. Learned.

Red flags can obviously be different for everybody. Like the guy who offered me Molly on the second date. For some people, that invitation might not have been a bad thing. Maybe some divorced moms would jump on that as a new experience. But for me it was a red flag. If something feels wrong to you, then don't ever feel bad about ending the conversation and unmatching the person.

My First Dick Pic and What to Do When You Get Yours

I learned the hard way (no pun intended) that some guys are not gentlemen via text. Take Marty, the serial online flasher, for example. I had been online for all of a few weeks when I matched with someone on Tinder who seemed to check all the boxes: intelligent, good job in advertising, close to my age, very good-looking. He seemed normal.

We texted on the app for a few days, and there was a definite connection. We made a date for a Saturday early-evening drink. We had texted a few times leading up to that day to confirm our plans, and I was about to leave my apartment to meet him when I got another message from him. I opened it to find multiple photos of his genitalia. Being new to this world, I was horrified.

I texted back something along the lines of, "Huh???"

He replied, "I thought you might want to see what could be in your future."

I did not meet Marty that day.

About a week later, I was on a fashion shoot, and I was talking about online dating with some of the other single women on the shoot. I mentioned my latest horror story, and one of them said, "Wait, that exact thing happened to my friend recently. And he fits the same description—what was his name?"

I replied, "Well, that's the thing; it's an uncommon name. His name was Marty." It was him. Marty the Penis Flasher was famous. A few weeks later, I was with a couple of friends and told my crazy tale from that day. One of my friends' jaw dropped. She said the same guy had done that to her friend. Marty was apparently the most notorious flasher of modern times.

Marty's antics are obviously an extreme example of what goes on behind closed doors and open apps. Most of the time, the exchanges with matches are "normal." I promise! I was lucky that this giant red flag reared its ugly head (again, no pun intended) *before* I actually met him in person. There are many times when this isn't the case. And think of how disappointing it is to go through an hour of "Where did you go to college? How many siblings do you have?" only to find out something like this at the end.

You might not be as lucky as I was to get the red flag before I walked out my door to meet Marty, the serial online flasher. But at least now you're prepared for the possibility! (I wish I could say this was the first and last time I received a "dick pic.")

When to Go IRL

After all the texting and dodging the flashers and red flags, how does one get to the point of asking a person out? Like the selfie and flirting over text, it takes practice. You may get turned down. In fact, I can almost guarantee it at least once. But this is all part of the journey. One thing I learned from online dating so much myself and watching this happen with my clients is that if you text for weeks on end without meeting, one or both of you feels let down or disappointed when you actually meet face-to-face.

There is too much buildup, and frankly, many people are much more charming over text than they are in real life. I got to the point toward the end of my online dating journey that I would flat-out say that I would not text for days on end. If we match and there's a remote connection, we make a date to see one another, even if it's a week out. We set a date and time to meet and then maybe check in here or there, but otherwise we wait to meet in person.

I learned this lesson the hard way. I had matched with someone on Bumble who lived in Paris but was in New York quite a bit for work and was even considering moving here. We made a date for when he was next in New York City. Then we proceeded to message for those two weeks every single day. He said all the right things, and I was completely charmed.

The night of our date I was so excited and nervous. He asked me to pick a restaurant in my neighborhood and said he would come to Brooklyn. I showed up to the dimly lit, romantic Italian restaurant in my 'hood and immediately knew that he was nothing like his texts and that his photos were at least a few years old. In his texts, he'd been sweet and interested in what was going on with me. In person, he was arrogant and aloof. I'm not sure what is worse: someone who clearly doesn't care what you have to say about yourself, or someone who pretends to. Now, I could see this guy, at least in person, was the former. A quality I'd sworn off long before. Still, I kept trying to see him in a positive light and even agreed to meet him a couple of nights later for dinner, thinking that maybe, just maybe, he was having an off night.

Two nights later, we met after work for a drink. He was as full of himself as he'd been the first night. Maybe even more. I was really, really disappointed. If he had asked me even one question about myself, maybe I would have gone to dinner with him that evening. But that didn't happen, so I excused myself after one drink.

I had put all of my *oeufs* into this French basket for the past two and a half weeks, and he was nothing like he'd seemed over text. I never forgot that lesson: ask the person out sooner than later and don't keep messaging endlessly in the interim.

Another example of how texting for too long before meeting can go horribly awry is my client Lulu, who worked in fashion in New York. She was texting for a couple of weeks with a guy she'd met on Bumble. By the time he got around to asking her out, she'd entered the busiest time in her industry—Fashion Month. They were texting incessantly during that whole time, checking in with each other every morning and texting a goodnight each night. When she got sick because of her crazy work schedule, he even dropped off soup with her doorman. Not once did they have even a FaceTime call throughout all of this.

Six weeks later, they finally had a date to meet in person. Six weeks of texting nonstop every day. Lulu met up with him at a local café . . . and he was wearing a cape and a top hat. The photos on his profile were of him wearing a turtleneck sweater and another with a T-shirt. Not wearing period costume. She was, needless to say, very disappointed. Not to mention feeling like she'd wasted six weeks of her dating life. He showed up to that date thinking it was a done deal. He'd already been talking about her and her son moving in with him to his two-bedroom Brooklyn apartment.

The moral of this story: ask the person out sooner than later. If she had asked him out herself, rather than waiting for him to do it, which then coincided with her busy work month, she wouldn't have been in that awkward situation.

Yet another example of why you should not text endlessly without at least a FaceTime call is my client Vera. She messaged with a guy from Canada for a couple of weeks. He was a DJ and said he could plan a trip to New York to play a few clubs and finally meet her in person. Vera was thrilled and agreed immediately. He was going to come right from the airport to her apartment before checking into his hotel. She was excited getting ready for his arrival. Her son was at his dad's for the weekend, she had a clean apartment, and she was ready to go out on the town with her (hopefully) new boyfriend. She buzzed him in, and when she opened her apartment door she wished she could close it again. He was more Overaged Club Kid than world-traveled DJ with his blue eyeliner and platform boots. At age fifty-one, he was not at all what she was expecting and not what he'd presented in his photos. She learned her lesson quickly: never make weekend plans with someone from out of town before at least having a video call.

You may be angry at me right now as I'm urging *you* to be the one to ask the guy out on a date. You might be thinking to yourself, *I've never asked someone out in my life*. Neither had I. But in my premarriage life, asking someone out was done face-to-face. Now, you can do it over a text. And what's the worst that can happen? They say no. And then you'll unmatch them and move on. You don't take it personally because they haven't even met the real you. They have seen a version of you through a few two-dimensional pixelated images and a handful of adjectives. This was always a comfort to me—and it should be to you too. If they knew the real me/you, they would definitely say yes.

Virtual Dating Tips

Since the pandemic, online daters have become not only open to a video call as a first date, but people are now feeling comfortable doing them. I know for myself, not only had I never FaceTimed with someone I was dating before, I had only FaceTimed a few times ever, with anyone. I started dating a guy who traveled a lot. He kept trying to get me to

FaceTime, and I kept putting it off and making excuses. When I finally caved, it took one or two calls to get comfortable, and then after that it became second nature. Here I go again—*practice makes perfect*.

I think video calls are a positive thing for a lot of online daters who, because of their schedules, wouldn't be able to go on many dates. Whether it's because they have children and getting time away is difficult or it's because they have a busy work schedule, virtual dating opens up many more opportunities to meet people.

Here are a few things to remember about doing live video calls:

- Try to plan a few in one evening. You may as well only have to get date-ready once a week rather than two or three. Think of it as virtual speed dating.
- Make sure you have decent lighting for your calls.
- Make sure your background is clean and not distracting.
- Practice with a friend first. Especially if you've never used Zoom or you've only used FaceTime a few times, you don't want to be on mute and not know how to unmute, and so on.
- It's difficult, but try not to keep looking at yourself and fixing your hair or fidgeting. Focus on your date.

Date Planning

If you haven't dated in a while, date planning can feel foreign. Who should pay? Where should you meet? How long should you stay? There are a lot of unknowns.

I like to tell clients about my experience handling the "who pays" question because for women it is always looming. For me, the first few months of dating, I would always offer to split the bill. Ninety-five percent of the time, the guy would decline. The subject came up at a party with another single woman, an acquaintance of mine, and she was shocked and practically scolded me. "You should never offer to pay," she said. "You're a single mom on a budget. If a man doesn't want to pay for you, then you shouldn't date him. None of my girlfriends ever offer to pay." I left the party wondering if she was right. Maybe I really didn't need to be offering to split the bill. Maybe I had been out of the dating scene for so long, I was out of touch.

The next few dates I went on, I tried her way and didn't even reach for my wallet. I thanked the person paying, of course. But something didn't feel right to me. Anyway, about a month later, I asked a guy I had dated a few times about it. I was genuinely curious how men felt about this practice and wanted to get to the bottom of it. He replied that he always appreciates, and pretty much expects, a woman to offer, but that he always says no. From then on,

I stuck with my original way. All this is to say, do what feels comfortable to you. And that might mean even bringing it up prior to the date if you feel strongly about it.

As far as the other two unknowns: *Where* you should go is where you know you will feel comfortable. Ideally somewhere you've been before, especially if you're really feeling nervous. Familiarity will give you comfort at least. *How long* you should stay should be decided ahead of time, at least in your own mind. You can always go into the date with plans already set afterward, such as meeting up with a friend or an appointment. That way you have your exit plan in place beforehand.

Game Time

You've matched. You've messaged. You've made an actual date. It's finally time for the IRL date. You've put together your FDU, so you know what to wear. Now it's time to get yourself pumped up. You will not cancel!

Let me tell you about my first date with someone I met online. Thinking about dating after being married for years can be intimidating, exciting, and frankly, straight-up terrifying. I was eager to start dating, as you may know by now. However, on the day of my first date, I was filled with anxiety. I even texted my date to tell him I may not be able to make it. Knowing I was extremely nervous, he saw right through my excuse and started telling me all the reasons why I should still come meet him.

The Only Box Worth Checking

There was this guy I met when I was just graduating college. He was tall (six foot one!), creative (a working photographer!), charming (he made me dinner on our first date!), and an intellectual (he had a subscription to *Harper's*!). Wow, did he check all my boxes. I felt like I'd hit the jackpot of mid-twenty-year-old guys. Not only that, but he lived two blocks away from me. He would make dinner for me almost every night while we drank wine and talked about art and music. We would go to galleries and museums together. We were *that* young city couple in love—at least to the outside world. I thought I had scored big-time.

In fact, I had scored so big-time, my boxes were so thoroughly checked, that when he asked me to marry him, I didn't hesitate. Of course, it would take me a few years, more than a decade really, to see my boxes for what they were: a false predictor of lifetime happiness. I really thought that I needed to be with someone creative. I was a creative person both professionally and personally, and I really thought that I wouldn't be happy with a noncreative type. My ex checked that box, as well as the "cool" box and the "tall" box and the "motivated" box. But what I wasn't paying attention to were all the signs that he was not a good partner for me. Sure, he "loved" me. But *saying* you love someone is a heck of a lot different than *showing* them. But *that* is another chapter. Actually, it's another book entirely.

I walked away from that marriage convinced that there's really only one box worth checking. It's the one that asks, *Do I feel good about myself when I'm with him/her?* End of story.

When it came to choosing him as my first IRL date, I was a little proud of myself for stepping outside my normal "type." And I very much had a type. My type was 1) creative, 2) intelligent, 3) motivated, and, of course, 4) tall. I had to force myself out of my comfort zone because I knew this "type" may not be the healthiest for me. After all, my "creative type" box had not served me well when I was dating the man who eventually became my ex-husband. I'd ignored many, many warning signs before we married, but he was so "my type." He'd ticked all my boxes. I'd had to learn the lesson of those false indicators the hard way. Now I knew, sometimes our boxes get in the way of seeing someone for who they truly are.

Let's call my first IRL date *Tony,* because when I described him to a friend, she thought I was talking about someone along the lines of Tony Soprano. He wasn't this at all, but my description of him may have had some similarities.

Tony embodied all the clichès of masculinity, unlike the metrosexual types I had always gone for in the past. He was a big, burly guy with a boyish smile. He had thick black hair and an even thicker Italian American New York accent. Unlike Tony Soprano, however, he was in fashion, not organized crime, and he grew up in Manhattan, not New Jersey, attending one of the fancy private schools in the city.

The day of our date, I paced around my apartment fretting about endless numbers of imaginary reasons why I shouldn't be doing this. What if I metaphorically (or literally) fell flat on my face? What if I had nothing to say, and we sat there in awkward silence? What if I choked on my drink and spit it out on the table? Yes, these thoughts actually went through my mind.

I called a friend who helped talk me off the ledge, and after hanging up the phone with her, I stared down my reflection in the mirror. I had to get my act together and get out the door. I put on some of my most pump-you-up music, put on my new jeans, put one foot in front of the other, and made it on the subway on my way to *my first date with someone I met online*.

Also newly separated from his wife of many years with two teenage daughters, Tony was a few months ahead of me with dating. To me that seemed like a veteran, so I let him lead the way with the date. He had suggested we meet for coffee in the city on a Saturday afternoon, which certainly seemed much less major than, say, a romantic dinner on a Friday night.

Our date was . . . fine. What had I been so worried about? I didn't trip and fall, literally or figuratively. I didn't spit out my coffee. And I was actually able to carry on a somewhat decent conversation. Despite my sweaty palms and racing thoughts, I somehow made it through with my self-esteem intact.

In fact, the date went pretty well. Sure, the whole time I was waiting for it to be over so I could go back to my apartment and sleep off the excitement mixed with anxiety. But the Band-Aid had been ripped off, which was a huge relief. I wasn't sure I was interested in Tony. After all, I knew he wasn't my type. But when he asked me out a second time, I said yes.

I went home feeling like I had just moved a mountain. I felt a huge sense of relief that the first date with a stranger I'd met on the internet was behind me. I'd made it through, and it wasn't all that bad.

Stomping All Over My Boxes, and It Was Freaking Awesome

I had a soft spot for Tony since he was my first actual date with someone I'd met online. We'd had a fine time on that first date. I'd accepted his invitation for a second date, but I doubted we'd make a love connection.

And yet. After talking for nearly two hours at a cute little French bistro in Soho, I started to see what a kind and grounded person he was. Not only that, but I found myself being really attracted to the fact that he was . . . nice.

When we left the café, he offered to walk me partway to my friend's house where I was going to a dinner party. I was supposed to bring dessert to the party and, as we parted ways, I mentioned to Tony I was going to stop at a gourmet market on the way. We said an awkward goodbye. I think we possibly even shook hands.

As I was walking away from him, I started wondering why he hadn't tried to kiss me. I was suddenly emboldened to text him and ask.

So I did. I sent a text saying exactly that: "Why didn't you kiss me?"

He responded immediately. "Stop where you are."

And just then, of all things, my phone died. I didn't know what to do at that point, so I went as planned into the market and picked out some ice cream and a pie and went to the checkout.

After paying, I turned around, and there he was, standing in front of me, smiling. He grabbed my hand and led me out of the store. He then turned to me and gave me the sexiest, most passionate kiss I'd had in *years*. We made out on the street for about forty-five minutes. I'm not exaggerating here.

I was late to the party. I felt like a teenager as I said some quick hellos to a few people and then snuck into my friend's office to call Tony. We couldn't stop texting each other. Within a few nights of texting, this turned into sexting. Something I knew absolutely *nothing* about at the time. What I did know? That this was the most damn fun I'd had in a long time.

It didn't work out with Tony in the end. It ultimately ended without drama, like with 95 percent of the other people I would date after meeting them online. But I'll always be grateful for our street love. And more important, I'll always be grateful that he showed me that having a type only limits you.

Ripping Off Your First-Date Band-Aid

Yes, I was so nervous about my first IRL date that I almost canceled, but getting through it, I knew for the first time that I was on the mend. I was going to be okay.

Are you ready to rip off your first-date Band-Aid? Here are my personal tips for approaching and preparing for first in-person dates:

1. Put on your favorite anthem of the moment to pump yourself up.

2. Make sure you know where you're going and how long it will take to get there so you're not stressed about being late.

3. Put on your FDU. You've already figured that out so you're not trying on your whole closet before a date.

4. Text your two best friends a selfie of you before you walk out the door to get some ego-boosting texts back.

Awkward Dating Rituals

-   *Greeting on a first date.* Hug? Wave? Handshake? Cheek kisses? All of these are normal, so go with what feels comfortable and most natural to you. The most important piece of this first greeting? Being confident and friendly.

-   *Wrapping up.* If you're ready for the date to end, a gentle signal is to finish your food or beverage and then politely decline more.

-   *Paying.* Paying, not paying, splitting, offering—all acceptable approaches. Be polite and do what makes you feel best and the most comfortable. For me, I liked

to offer to pay. Ninety-five percent of the time, the guy
did not take me up on it.

- *Saying goodbye.* Whether you're looking for a kiss or
looking to avoid one at all costs, make your intentions
clear in your body language. And, as always, as long as
you are confident and friendly, even the most awkward
goodbyes can end on a warm note.

Keep Dating

After Tony, I tried dating men from age twenty-six to fifty-
six and everything in between. I dated a teacher, a banker,
a film student, a model, a CEO, a tennis instructor, a real
estate broker, a furniture designer, a lawyer, a hotelier, a
fashion designer, and an advertising executive. I dated
men from the United States, Canada, Peru, England, Ja-
pan, Iran, Panama, France, Italy, Jamaica, India, Switzer-
land, South Africa, and Israel. And I dated a woman.

I mean, why not? I've always had good relationships
with women—my mom, my grandmother, two sisters, lots
of female friends. I've always related better to women.
And I did have the occasional experimental encounters in
college. I also know of several other female friends who
dated women after their divorce from a man. It's not

unusual and, in fact, it's more common than you would think. I was curious.

I ran it by one of my oldest and dearest friends, who also happens to be a therapist, to ensure that I wasn't using this as a defense mechanism to not be hurt by men anymore. Knowing me and my history and my marriage, she gave me the go-ahead. Not merely the go-ahead but her complete support of my new path. Who knows? Maybe I was going to meet the Abby to my Glennon.

I was going to date a woman. With my therapist friend's blessing, I immediately went onto one of my dating apps and toggled my preference. I was nervous but also feeling very empowered by my decision. After messaging with a few people, I had a connection with one of them. We made a date to meet for a drink in the city. This. Is. Happening.

I was the first to arrive at the restaurant bar, one I had been to years before with my ex-husband. I ordered a drink and nervously waited. She arrived and was taller than I expected, and at first, I was worried she wasn't my type, but after talking for a while, I started to change my mind. She was also newly separated from her husband and was always equally attracted to women and was giving it a try. We were both new to this so it felt even safer in case it didn't work out. I felt like we were both trying something new, postdivorce.

After an hour of chatting and getting to know each other, she walked me to my subway line. We awkwardly said our goodbyes and she asked if I would like to do this again. Yes. Yes, I would.

After dating for about six weeks, which meant seeing each other about five times, I decided that, while I was physically attracted to her and other women, I didn't know if I was sexually attracted to women. Is there a difference? I don't know, but what I do know is that I can honestly say that I did not "style my soul mate." I really expanded my horizons and tried every angle. There is a freedom in that, and online dating provides a great opportunity to take the first steps. Keep going with your dating journey. Keep stepping outside your "type" and your "boxes." See what you learn about yourself and have some fun doing it.

One Fine Date

As someone who encourages and believes in online dating, there's one aspect of it that drives me crazy.

There's a reason why we only hear about the people who meet their soul mate on Tinder and get married, or the date where the guy showed up twenty minutes late, ten years older than his pics, thirty pounds heavier, and talked about his antique hatchet collection for forty-five minutes. Because those stories are the most fun to hear about! Would your friends want to hear about the so-so date where you both shook hands amicably after one drink, and you went home and watched Netflix?

Not all online dating is dramatic and crazy. It's simply that those experiences are the only ones we hear about. You can meet someone who is neither Mr. Right nor Mr. Murderer. Most of the time, it goes more like this: you meet someone great, there are no sparks, and you become friends instead. That's what I experienced, and most of my clients have experienced the same. So, if the "online dating is too crazy" mantra keeps going through your head, please don't let that hold you back. There are people out there just like you. Ask your friends to tell you about the mundane dates they have been on.

The vast majority of dates will be "fine." In my amateur field study, most people are nice, normal people. Not necessarily exciting but not horrible. You'll know a little bit more about humanity after you've been online dating for a while. Generally, most people aren't as funny as Jon Stewart or as handsome as Ryan Gosling. Every date can be a learning experience *if you want it to be*. These dates will teach you something about yourself—and about human nature, the different ways people live, occupations and cultures you may not have known much about before. Even when the chemistry isn't there, it's usually nice to talk to someone, to hear their story. If a date is just "fine," that doesn't mean it was a failure or a waste of time. I would insert more anecdotes from clients here, but I don't hear much about the "nice" dates. Only the amazing ones and the strange ones.

Date from Hell

This does happen, but way less often than you'd imagine. If you do have a bad date, chalk it up to being part of the online dating experience. We've all had them at one point or another. It's nothing you did. Don't blame yourself! My suggestions are to go home, put your favorite music on, and journal about it. Then call a friend and embellish the story and have a good laugh.

How to Turn Someone Down for Another Date

I really do encourage you to go on second and maybe even third dates with someone, even if you don't feel the thunder and lightning of love at first sight. Still, there are going to be times when going on another date with a person is simply not something you're willing to do. So, how do you turn the person down politely?

- *Don't ghost!* You wouldn't want someone to do this to you. It can be tempting to avoid the person and simply drop them without a word, but in the end, you will feel so much better if you are mature and communicate in an up-front way instead of leaving the person hanging.
- *Use this tried-and-true script:*
  You had a nice time and thank them.
  You didn't feel a romantic spark.
  You wish them the best.
- *Personalize the message so that it's in your voice and also speaks personally to the person you're turning down.* For example, you might want to tell the person you hope he or she has a good time on an upcoming trip or best wishes with whatever endeavor he or she may have discussed, such as a new job, running a marathon, writing a book, and so on.

Losing Your Postdivorce Virginity

Let's talk about another Band-Aid that might need to be ripped off. If you've already been here, then you know the emotions that go along with "the first time" with someone new. It really does, in many ways, feel like the first time: you're incredibly self-conscious, you don't know what you're doing (I mean, if you've been with one person for the last twenty-plus years, you get used to certain ways things are done), and you may wonder what this means to the relationship.

My personal journey to get to this point is comical at best and pathetic at worst. I think I may have mentioned already how I couldn't stop thinking about men and sex? I was trying very hard to make this happen. The First Guy, a.k.a. TD&EH, as you may remember from chapter 1, was an ex from long ago who looked me up when he was trying to make an open marriage where there wasn't one. That ended with me sending him on his way.

The Second Guy I met, a.k.a. Tony, I thought would be a good candidate, but he had recently come out of a twenty-four-year marriage. He basically became terrified to be alone with me, because he was so not ready, and I'd made it clear I was. I kept throwing myself at him, but he was still too devastated by his ex-wife cheating on him. He'd discovered her Ashley Madison account, and when he confronted her, she decided to leave him. Within a month, he gently broke things off with me—no drama but still no sex.

The Third Guy was the first time I was set up by a friend. He was a creative, artistic type and also a single dad. I was in. We met for a drink in my neighborhood. I didn't think there was a spark, but I did enjoy his company. For our second date, he offered to come to my place and make dinner.

He arrived at 7:30 p.m. We were done eating by ten, but then he stayed until 3:00 a.m. . . . talking.

I thought I was giving lots of signals and making it very clear that I was interested. But apparently not. When he left, after we'd spent seven and a half hours together, he gave me an awkward peck on the cheek. The next day he texted what a great time he'd had and could we do it again the following week? Hmmm. *So, he's interested but extremely shy?* I still didn't know.

The next time, he came over with wine and stayed until the wee hours again. But, alas, just another peck on the cheek. It was becoming a joke among my friends—I was quite literally throwing myself at these men, and they wouldn't reciprocate. I still don't have an explanation other than I practically had an invisible "I want to get laid" sign on my forehead. Apparently, that was a turnoff to many men.

Complaining to yet another single friend about my unfortunate situation, she had an idea. She had a guy friend for me, Fourth Guy. He had recently broken up with a girlfriend of five years. He was a handsome professor and seemed very sure of himself. He was also looking to rip off the same Band-Aid. My friend kept reminding me that this was not a setup because we were so wrong for one another, but for a one-night fling, it would be perfect.

She connected us, and we made a date for drinks, conveniently a few blocks from my apartment. She was right that he wasn't my type personality-wise, but Fourth Guy was definitely easy on the eyes. I also felt, because he was a friend of a friend, it was somehow safer. We went back to my place, both very nervous, and well, let's just say he was a little too nervous. It didn't happen. Again. But we were both very respectful and parted ways after that night amicably.

Guy Number Five was from work, a much-younger-than-me millennial who had been flirty with me since I started working there. And maybe the topic of me losing my proverbial virginity might have gotten around my co-workers. There was a large group of us who would go out after work, and occasionally he was in the mix. One Friday night, Guy Five and I outlasted everyone else, mainly because there was major chemistry between us. He walked me to wait for my Uber and started kissing me. In my head I was like, *This is it! I'm finally going to make this thing happen*! Ten minutes into this on-the-street passionate make-out session (which was becoming a regular occurrence in my newly single life), he told me he'd recently started seeing someone—his own age—whom he really liked, and it had gotten serious pretty fast. *Ugh.*

I could tell it was eating him up. And although the whiskey was telling Guy Five to go home with me, his heart was telling him to go home. I felt for him and made up an excuse that I had to be up early anyway. He was always very sweet. And he is actually still with the girl he liked almost five years later. I am happy to report that there are men out there who don't stray, no matter how tempted they may be.

Okay, so where were we? Oh, right.

The number of guys I'd thrown myself at: five.

Number of times I'd had sex: zero.

By this point, I was starting to think something was wrong with me. And the joke among my friends became less funny to me. I took a few weeks off thinking maybe I was giving off some needy vibe, and I needed to reset.

When I went back onto one of the dating apps, I started messaging with a single dad who was only a neighborhood away from me. "The same train line!" he said. We went out twice, and there was a major connection. We texted all the time, waiting for our next date. I felt like I'd not only found someone to lose my "virginity" to, I'd found someone I could actually date! Our conversations both by text and over the phone flowed so easily. I even told him of my so-called dilemma, and he was ready to oblige.

Our third date was coming up. Neither of us had our kids that weekend, so it could be on a Saturday night. I packed a change of clothes because we were feeling that comfortable and knew that, after our date, I would go home with him to spend the night.

I felt awkward and very self-conscious at first, but not for long. Everything went much better than what I'd built up in my mind. Without going into explicit details, because that's a different book entirely, sex was exactly how I remembered it being with someone new—fun, nervous, exciting. Just like riding a bike.

Afterward, we talked late into the night about one another and our pasts and our personalities. He even made mention that he would like to discuss going off the dating app and seeing where this might go. The next morning he went out and got bagels. I looked around, and I was further impressed by the fact that I liked his apartment and his taste in furniture. But when he got back, I could sense he wanted some alone time. I made an excuse that I needed to get some things done at home before my kids got back.

I didn't hear from him at all that day. My gut told me something was off. That night, after my kids went to bed, I went onto the dating app where we'd met and I noticed he wasn't on there. I searched a little more and saw he'd gone back on under a different username (on this app you didn't have to use your real name). He'd also rewritten his profile using some of the exact wording that I had used to describe him the night before. I had discussed how talented I thought he was after seeing some of his paintings. I'd commented on his sense of humor and joked about his taste in music. He made sure to include all of these details in his new profile bio. It really stung.

I felt totally duped. I texted him, and all he could say was, "I think I want to get back together with my ex-girlfriend," whom he'd run into that day. Which was an excuse, of course, because why would he still be on the dating app? I was devastated. I felt the way a young girl must feel when she finally decides to do this, to have sex for the first time, and then the guy never calls again.

I have to say, though, looking back, I made it a bigger deal in my mind and during the time leading up to it than it needed to be. If you're like me and feel terrified of this moment, fear not—it can actually be fun.

After this first time, I gave myself permission going forward to do it for me and not for anyone else. I give you permission to do the same. I was not going to care what society told me I should want or what I should do. And I hope that you do the same. I was enjoying myself and my freedom.

Sex is a natural, exciting part of dating after divorce. It's fun to talk about and fun to think about. Let yourself enjoy the experience without thinking too, too hard about it. Here's the obvious thing we all know but that is worth repeating: great sex doesn't always lead to a great relationship, just as online dating doesn't always end in a happily-ever-after love match. But sometimes it does. Be yourself, be open, enjoy the process.

A Frank Conversation About Creating a Healthy Sex Life While Dating

- *You are normal.* Forget what society, TV, and the media say about "traditional" sex habits. Embrace your sexuality and do what makes you happy and comfortable. There are no rules!
- *Communicate.* Challenge yourself to openly communicate with your partner and constantly check in—you both will benefit.
- *Enjoy!* Listen to your desires, listen to your partner, and enjoy all that sex and intimacy has to offer. It doesn't matter what you *used to do* or what you *used to like* or what your previous partner liked or told you—it's all about YOU *now*.

Ghosting, Zombieing, and Haunting: Are You Scared?

Ahh, the dreaded G word: ghosting. Unfortunately, if you go online to date, ghosting will happen to you at some point. It could be in a minor way: after a day of texting back and forth, the person stops texting you for no apparent reason and unmatches you on the dating app, never to be heard from again. Or in a more major way: you have dated for a couple of months, and they simply stop answering your texts. That actually happened to a client of mine, but it's very rare. Minor, major, and everything in between, ghosting has happened to me, my clients, and my friends at least once during their online dating adventures.

Kara, a divorced client of mine in New York City, had a heartbreaking experience when she met a downtown divorced dad of three, Sandy, on Hinge. On their first date, he told her that he had broken up with his girlfriend of two years. He and his ex-girlfriend had started a fitness business together that was wildly successful. He talked a lot about the business and his ex, who he insisted was solely a business partner at this point. But he seemed very interested in Kara, so she continued to go on several more dates with him. Their fourth date was spending New Year's Eve together, and when I spoke to her the next day she was ecstatic about how things were moving along. She thought she had met someone who could be a long-term partner.

Several days later, she texted me that she had not heard from Sandy since the morning of New Year's Day when he left her apartment. She texted him and didn't hear back. Weeks went by without hearing another word. Kara went on the Instagram account of the fitness instructor (Sandy's ex and business partner) and saw that she'd posted a few photos of her and Sandy together again, holding hands.

Kara was devastated and confused. This is obviously a worst-case scenario, but something to be aware of. Of course, now Kara admits she saw the red flags but chose to ignore them. She didn't trust her gut.

The main thing with ghosting is to remember not to take it personally. This has everything to do with the ghoster and not the ghostee. It's the easy way out. It's completely unfair. And you will probably do it to someone else too.

I encourage you not to ghost anyone. It's part of the reason that online dating gets such a bad rap. If very few people ghosted, it wouldn't be so dreaded and more people would feel good about getting online to date. Think twice before blowing someone off. If nothing else, text the person with the following script: "I'm very sorry, but I have decided to take a break from dating [or another appropriate reason]. It's nothing you did, I'm just not in a place right now to move forward."

You don't want ghosting to happen to you, so don't do it to others. Be open and up front, and you can't go wrong. Positivity and honesty are key in successful online dating.

Can you guess what zombieing is? It's kind of like ghosting, but it involves one extra step: the person who dissed you tries to come back from the grave. The "zombie" seemingly disappeared from your life, out of nowhere, but then popped back in your life with a text or a "like" on social media. The worst offender might match with you on another app. Unless they have a believable but out-of-this-world apology, it should be a big fat No.

Haunting, a relative of the above two dating woes, is when a ghost from a previous relationship or fling somehow gets stuck in your online realm. They occasionally like your posts or watch your Instagram stories but don't reach out or ask you out. The best response to a haunting? Ignore it and hope it will fade away.

There's constantly new lingo popping up when it comes to online dating—too much to keep track of. Some of the lingo is funny, and some, like "catfishing" (you show up to a date and the person looks nothing like their photos) and "breadcrumbing" (when someone strings you along while also dating other people), hit a little close to home if you've experienced whatever it is personally. When you're on the apps or messaging and you see a term, phrase, acronym, or emoji you don't recognize, ask a friend or Google it before responding. There are some you don't want to get wrong.

Trust Your Gut

Even if there are no obvious red flags, your intuition is the strongest ally you have. One thing all my married friends kept saying to me was, "You're going to go out with a total stranger to a bar??" I had one close friend, Larissa, who would proceed to worry about me all night, scared I would wind up chained in a basement somewhere. Larissa would make me text her when I got home (which I did—albeit not always alone). But I will always love her for worrying so much about me.

I didn't have any fears about meeting people. My argument to her was, "Do you think it was any better in our twenties when we met some guys at a bar and gave them our number to meet them at another bar another night? We didn't know them either!"

Still, I would always plan to meet my dates in a public, bustling place. There was only one time I felt the situation was a little dicey, and that was the guy who suggested we do Molly together when all I wanted was dinner out. After he kept texting me, I simply blocked him. It wasn't a big deal. As I said: trust your gut.

Every now and then I would get a weird feeling—*and it was always right on the money*. I've also had clients show me exchanges where something felt off, and I would read them and totally agree. When you run those conversations by someone else, it's usually pretty glaring to an outside person, so trust yourself but also feel free to show the messages to someone else for confirmation. If something feels uncomfortable, then it's usually not quite right.

This is a time in your life when you have to learn to trust your instincts, something we all should have been doing in our twenties and—at least in my case—didn't. If you're saying to yourself right now, "What if I don't have gut feelings?" You do. You just need to listen more closely.

Some situations when your gut is talking to you:

- You're sexting with someone and everything seems great, until he texts something that gives you a twinge of doubt—that's your intuition talking.
- You get a text or a call saying he can't make the date you made and you get a weird feeling about it—that's your gut telling you he's probably making an excuse.
- You finally sleep with him and the next morning, something feels off. That's also your gut telling you something *is* off. I'm speaking from experience here.
- Listen to your gut, your instincts, your hunch. Trust me. They know you better than you know yourself.

Let Yourself Be Vulnerable

Something a lot of people have a very hard time with: vulnerability. But I feel it's key to letting someone get to know you. Showing a side of you that can let your guard down and be, well, vulnerable. It goes a long way in relationships in general, but especially in dating. People want and need an opening. A way in. It could be something you've never told anyone or something that changed you or how you view life. Or it could be about finding your true passion in something unexpected, something revealing another side of you. I'm not suggesting you talk about a deep dark secret on the first date, of course. The timing has to feel right, and you have to have some level of trust. But to form a deeper connection with someone, showing a level of vulnerability is important.

Go on More Than One Date

Most people have a side of themselves they show the world—it's the same side they show on first dates, only even more polished. But we all have layers to us, that onion metaphor where we have to peel away the layers to get to our true personality. Getting to the center of the onion can take a few dates or a few years. I wasn't sure My Perfect Match (MPM) was a match for me until date number four. I kept going out with him because I knew that he was a nice person. It took four dates to feel any chemistry and a few more to know we actually had incredible chemistry.

When my clients call me the day after a first date and tell me, "It was fine, but there was no chemistry," I want to reach through the phone and shake them. How many times have you gone out with someone new and you come home thrilled because the two of you had "major chemistry," only to go out a couple more times before he or she blows you off or you cool off? See? Your feelings after date number one cannot be trusted.

It wasn't until we were dating for a couple of months that I discovered that MPM a) had some seriously cute (and sexy) dance moves and b) we could crack each other up with the most ridiculous nicknames for each other. I soon started thinking I had met my soul mate.

I encourage my clients to go out on more than one or two dates with someone—assuming the baseline of being a nice person—before making a call on whether that person is right for you. You never know what awesome sense of humor or something else that you're attracted to might surface after the person gets more comfortable around you.

Many of us are still stuck in this thought that there is an ideal person you will meet someday who will check all the boxes. The first box is usually sense of humor. We all think we're funny and deserve someone as funny as we are. The second box is that he should be tall. If I had a dollar for every time a client says she wants someone tall, I'd be retiring right now. The third is usually something like smart or successful. I know all your boxes, because I had the same ones . . . at first. We have all created boxes since we started being attracted to other people. Screw the boxes! Tear down your boxes! Think outside your damn boxes!

Your next ideal mate may not look/talk/walk like you are expecting and may not have the job/kid situation/location that (you think) you want. In modern dating, you have to be open to meeting lots of different types of people. And the person may not check any of your so-called important boxes. You can always find some flaw in another person. The most important thing is how that person makes you feel. This is something I wish I had been more in touch with when I was young.

At the end of the day, or life, it doesn't matter how cool people are or how much money they make or how much you love their friends and family or what college they went to or what music they listen to or how much they read or what they cook. It matters how they look at you and treat you. When you are around them, do you feel awesome? Or do you feel insecure and bad about yourself? This may all be obvious to some people, but to most of us, unfortunately, it's not. It's something that a lot of us choose to overlook because we get caught up in a certain image of ourselves and our future fantasy life. I'll even go so far as to say your boxes may be making you judgy. They may even be making you snobby. And they are definitely causing you to miss out on potentially great partners.

I encourage all of my clients to keep a *really* open mind when it comes to dating. Did I go into online dating thinking, *I want to meet a man who works way too much who is only in New York halftime*? Of course not. But if I had ruled out MPM based on those two things, I would now not be with this awesome person who is my perfect partner. I'm not saying *he* is perfect. But he is perfect *for me*. Is there a perfect match out there for you? In all likelihood there's probably more than one perfect person, but you'll never know if you don't keep at it.

Dig In, Don't Dabble

Online dating isn't easy, but if you screw all those boxes, keep an open mind, and put the effort in, it can be rewarding. My friends used to say to me, "You're so lucky you met MPM." But I would quickly correct them: "No. I'm not lucky. I'm diligent." I put in more than two years of online dating, and it certainly wasn't all romantic dinners and street kissing. There were some jilted feelings, confusing moments, uncomfortable sexual encounters, and angry texts. There were also eye-opening revelations, late nights filled with interesting conversation, exploring my own sexuality, and, yes, street kisses too.

If you half-heartedly post a profile, check it only once every couple of weeks, and don't follow up with matches, you won't get very far. Sure, you may have a few decent dates here and there, but it's unlikely you will find your dream date or feel satisfied doing it that way.

If you put some effort into your profile, keep up the work, and then have a few bad experiences and throw in the towel, telling yourself something along the lines of "Online dating doesn't work," that also won't get you very far. You need to be ready to take the bad with the good. The online flashers with the George Clooneys. Chalk up the unpleasant dates to learning more about what you *don't* want.

Which leads me to a reminder for you to check that list of What You Want and What You Don't Want every now and again. Check back through your journal and read about past dates and mistakes you made and learn from them. Put them behind you and move forward with positivity. In short, be intentional about online dating.

What started as me wanting sex turned into me meeting new friends, which then became me meeting my absolute best friend and life partner. To do it, I had to make myself vulnerable, which was scary after the relationship I'd left, but I took the risk and it was worth it. If I can do it, so can you.

Swipe #1,534—I Finally Meet My Match

Two-plus years, hundreds of swipes, thousands of messages, and close to one hundred IRL dates later, I was really, finally, actually ready to meet a long-term partner. I learned a lot on all those dates: about myself, but also about what was really important to me in a partner. So many things I previously thought were important simply weren't. And I discovered some qualities were absolutely not negotiable: I wanted him to be respectful and emotionally intelligent.

I had distilled it down to these two must-have qualities by much trial and error, as you know. These were important—no, these were *vital*—especially to me, because they were qualities that had been lacking in my marriage. It wasn't until I was away from my marriage that I realized how much, as a woman, in these times, I really needed these qualities in my life. I wanted this person to be respectful of me, my views, my career path. I wanted someone who believed in me and my abilities. I also wanted the person to be in touch with emotions, not just in himself, but with my emotions as well.

I had just ended things with a guy whom I dated for a few months. Correction: he'd ended things with me. It was nothing personal—he simply didn't want to be with someone long term who had kids. I remember leaving his apartment, disheartened. I took an Uber to meet up with some friends who had already been out for hours and took advantage of their tipsy state. I poured my heart out to them about being so over dating, so over swiping, so over all of it. They encouraged me, as girlfriends do, and said all the things a girl needs to hear when someone dumps her. Feeling somewhat convinced that I wasn't doomed to being on dating apps for the rest of my days, I went home and did what any self-respecting divorcee does: I opened up Tinder and swiped away until the wee hours.

Shortly after that, I decided it was time to get serious about the search. I needed to manifest the right guy (by this point, I'd determined it would be a guy) as I did with the Africa trip. I took out my journal and wrote down all the qualities and traits I really, truly wanted. I got specific. Your list might look something like this:

- Has hobbies of his own
- Likes being with my kids
- Enjoys traveling
- Likes being active as well as lazing around
- Thinks I'm funny

Over the next few weeks, I felt like I was getting closer and closer to the right thing. As I went on more dates, with my new focus, I had better and better dates, with better and better people for me. One notion that had stayed with me those couple of years, that I'm grateful for, is the feeling that I *would* meet the right person someday. I believed it. I lived like it was going to happen. I manifested it. I read and reread my list of qualities. I kept up with the dating apps.

A random weeknight without my daughters, lying on my couch in my sweatpants, in for the night at only 7:00 p.m., I opened my Tinder app and started to swipe. My index finger hovered over the profile of a guy. I swiped through all of his photos and realized he had picked the best one for the first photo (bonus points for that!). The rest were either with sunglasses or where I couldn't really get a sense of who he was. But that first photo was a good one. It was a selfie in a mirror, which normally guys his age can't quite get right. He later told me that was sheer luck and that he probably hadn't taken a selfie since. He wasn't smiling in the photo, but he also wasn't serious. He had a content look on his face, like he was confident but not cocky. He had on a shirt that fit him very well (more bonus points!). There was something about that one photo (which I luckily screenshotted and still have four years later).

His bio read like a résumé: where he was from, where he went to college, and other mundane stuff like that. He also explained that he lived between New York City, Washington, DC, and Central America, which seemed exciting. Later I would realize it was less "exciting" and more just time apart.

Despite the bio being on the boring side, I was intrigued. I swiped right and got the notification that we were a match—which meant he had already swiped right on me. Within three seconds, he messaged me something along the lines of "Hey, how are you?" and I responded with "That was the fastest response time ever." And the banter started from there. After just a few exchanges, he asked what I was doing that night because he was leaving town the next day. That would usually be a bit of a red flag to ask for a date that same night (someone who just wanted to hook up), but he seemed nice. I said I was in for the night, and he suggested coffee in the morning.

These were my days of working at a downtown photo studio nearly every day as an art director. I agreed to meet him before work as long as he could meet somewhere near the studio. He immediately sent me a place to meet and we agreed on 8:15 a.m.

The next morning, I got a little more dressed up and wore a little bit more makeup than usual. I arrived at the café he'd chosen and went to the counter to order a matcha. MPM arrived a few minutes later and said he'd ordered the same thing. We chatted for a while, talking about the usual things one does on a first date, and he offered to walk me to work from there. When I got to the door of the building, MPM asked if we could go to dinner the next week when he got back from his trip. I wasn't sure if I "liked him-liked him," but I was willing to give it a go. He seemed like a good person. I wasn't sure if he was my "type," but I reminded myself we don't do that anymore.

Over the next few weeks, we texted a lot. (I would later find out, not nearly enough, according to MPM.) We also managed to see each other two more times for dinner in between his work trips. I still wasn't sure I was attracted to him, but he was a really nice person who asked a lot of questions about me, which was the exact opposite of most New York guys who love to talk about themselves. It was refreshing to say the least.

On our third date, MPM was telling me he had to go to London in the next couple of weeks and asked if I wanted to go with him. I was surprised that he would ask when we had barely even kissed goodnight at this point. I told him I'd have to think about it. By the time I got home, I had already convinced myself that it would be crazy to go on a trip to London with a practical stranger.

But he was persistent. MPM told me that it seemed like I could use a weekend of pampering. A weekend away, not thinking about my still-intense divorce situation. London was one of his favorite cities, and he wanted to take me to his favorite restaurants and shops. MPM then even told me he would get me my own hotel room so there wasn't any pressure on me. That new information was tempting. Still, I said I'd think about it.

I mentioned it to my mom, expecting her, of all people, to tell me that I was being smart turning down such a ridiculous proposition from a near stranger. Instead, she said, "Why not, if you'll have your own hotel room?" Um, Mom, are you feeling okay? But also, it was just what I wanted to hear. I wanted permission to go to London with this guy I had met three times. It would be an adventure.

And it coincided with days that my kids would be with their dad.

I texted MPM to tell him I'd changed my mind about London—I would like to join him. He wrote back immediately asking what had made me change my mind. I joked that my mom had given me permission. And then I told him the actual reasons: 1) I liked the idea of being pampered, or rather, someone wanting to pamper me, and 2) with his busy travel schedule and my kid schedule, it would take a long time to get to know each other. This three-day weekend would accelerate things, for good or for bad. As I put it, we'll either know we want to continue dating or we'll both run away screaming after that weekend. He was thrilled with this point, which made it even more clear I had made the right decision.

Leading up to the trip, MPM was not afraid of letting me know just how excited he was that I would join him for the last few days of his trip. I found it super endearing that he wasn't "playing it cool." He texted me the hotel where I would be staying. It looked so nice! He texted me my flight info, which he'd upgraded with his miles. He texted me that he was so looking forward to the weekend. And I was too.

Those three days in London were probably the best days of my life. It sounds cheesy, but I was so content. I wasn't worried about my divorce or my lawyer bills that were piling up. I wasn't even missing my daughters—a first for me! Needless to say, we hit it off. The London trip was a success. MPM and I have been together since.

For two and a half years before meeting MPM, I'd swiped on hundreds of people and gone out with a good portion of them. I got frustrated and gave up dozens of times. I wanted to throw in the towel on online dating. But I didn't. I believed I would meet someone, so I kept at it.

I firmly believe that if I had met MPM one year before, I probably would not have ended up with him. I would have assumed there was "no chemistry" and stayed friends. And if I had met him two years before, I would have sabotaged it completely because he was "too nice."

I had learned so much about online dating, sure. But I had also learned an incredible amount about myself throughout all of it. I learned that I *didn't* like to listen to EDM during dinner and that I was over building forts for my kids. I learned that I *did* like to paint by YouTube videos with my daughters and that I liked to cook. But, of course, the most important of all is that I learned that I liked myself. She was fun. She was talented in some areas, and smart in others. She was a good mom and friend. She was deserving of someone who appreciated her for who she was and treated her as such.

And I realized I had collected a wealth of information in those two-plus years. I finally followed all of my dating advice. With MPM, I acted on all that I'd learned:

1. Going out with someone who was not "my type." Or so I thought.

2. Pushing myself to go out with someone more than once or twice to see if there was more to that person. And boy, was I glad I went on those third and fourth dates.

3. Using my new language and communication skills. I was up front and honest every step of the way with MPM.

4. Trusting my gut. Most importantly, I learned to listen to my inner voice. I trusted my instinct to go to London. And at that point, I knew in every fiber, muscle, and blood vessel of my being that he was right for me.

The point is that I didn't luck out. I was diligent and determined to meet someone. Not just anyone. But the *right* someone for me. I figured out the art of online dating.

Style Your Swiping Cheat Sheet

- Try all the apps and see which one you like best.
- Start conversations and go on dates with people who aren't your "type." Forget all of your "boxes." The only box that really matters: how the person makes you feel when you're with them.
- Don't be afraid to start messaging with someone. Communicating doesn't mean you're committed to going on an IRL date. It's just talking.
- In text/app conversations, message with only a few people at a time to stay focused. Compliment personality, not looks. Find common ground, be positive, and focus on the person's unique qualities. Ask questions! Keep messages short and simple. Reread your message before hitting send.
- If you're not sure what an acronym or emoji means, ask a friend or Google it to avoid miscommunication.
- Pay attention to red flags and trust your gut.
- If you're at all interested in a person you're messaging with, consider meeting in person, or doing a FaceTime call, sooner rather than later to avoid wasting time.
- Decide how you want to handle the "who pays" question for dates ahead of time. Plan dates for a

place where you feel comfortable. Set an end time
for dates.

- Keep dating, knowing most dates will be . . . fine.
Keep going.
- To turn someone down for another date, avoid
ghosting that person. Instead, personalize the message,
say you had a nice time, you didn't feel a romantic
spark, and you wish that person the best.
- When it comes to ripping off the sex Band-Aid, try
not to make too big a deal of it. Embrace your
sexuality, communicate with your partner, and enjoy
yourself!
- Go on more than one date with a person. Sudden
chemistry doesn't always lead to long-term chemistry.
Sometimes it takes a few dates to start to get to know
someone.
- Dig in, don't dabble. Putting in minimal effort will not
lead to great matches. Updating your profile,
messaging with matches, and going on dates will help
you get closer and closer to better matches for you.
Continue to journal on your Wants and Don't Wants as
you learn more and meet more people. Let yourself be
vulnerable with people you're interested in and see
what develops.

- Believe you will meet someone. Live like you know it's going to happen. Read and reread your Wants and the qualities (qualities, not superficial types or boxes) you are looking for in a person. Stay active on the apps.
- Take a chance on someone . . . they just may be the right someone for you.

Acknowledgments

I have to start by thanking my best friend, partner, and forever my biggest fan, Yoav Gery. If it weren't for him, I wouldn't have started Style My Profile, and therefore wouldn't be writing this book about my experiences in the crazy world of post-divorce online dating. Yoav, you so believe in me and appreciate all of me.

Tied for number one acknowledgement is my mother, Sally Judge. You brought me into this world, and without you, I couldn't have made it through those long years of my divorce and since then. You supported me more than you will ever know. You have talked me off many ledges and are generally my human version of a Xanax. Thanks, Mom.

To my two incredible daughters, Hayden and Story. You are already truly super humans, and I'm so lucky to call you both my offspring. You are always my inspiration to keep going: keep writing, keep working on myself, keep being strong. I want to be, and hope that I am, a role model to both of you, like my own mother was to me.

My agent, Amy Hughes, who cold-called me when she saw the article in the *New York Times* about Style My Profile. Amy not only saw the potential of a book on modern online dating by a divorcee but also saw that there was a story behind my post-divorce metamorphosis. She believed in my business and my personal journey of reinvention.

To the Harper Horizon publishing team: Andrea Fleck-Nisbet, Amanda Bauch, and John Andrade, who must be the most patient publishing team for first-time writers ever. It was truly a pleasure to work with all of you. Thank you for believing in my story.

My editor and friend Danielle Pergament, who was way too busy to be helping me with this book, but since we've been friends for twenty years, did it anyway. You helped me find my voice, and without you this book might be one run-on cliché!

To my final-round editor, Bessie Gantt, who has the nicest way of telling you that something makes you sound douchey. Thank you for seeing the potential of this book despite having never been anywhere near the online dating world!

To the genius and one of nicest people I've ever known, my content director, producer, and right-hand woman,

Katherine Paulsen. Without her picking up the slack on everything else, I wouldn't have finished this book in the time that I did.

To Carmindy, who was one of my cheerleaders from when I first launched Style My Profile. To Malia Mills, who was the first to tell me all of my experiences should be a book.

To Laura Stockman, the illustrator and graphic designer for this book, who turns around things quicker than you can say "illustration."

Jocelyn Kaye, for being my lifeline, personal style advisor, therapist, and coconspirator, especially during my divorce, but forever and always. Larissa Thomson, for being a best friend who always wants to help solve your problems, even if they aren't solvable! Tricia Stahel Smith, for always being my voice of reason, in all areas of my life, and also for being my design advisor for all things Style My Profile. Kate Collins, for helping me fine-tune the style archetypes section and for always being up for a vent session. Kady Davies and Karen Kozlowski, for sharing their dating war stories with me when I was having writer's block. Lida Moore, for believing in me and hiring me when I needed it most, without even knowing how she was uplifting this broken woman. My dear friend Karen Duggan, for being my first and forever best friend—you are like a sister to me.

And last but not least, to my two sisters, Arian and Kristina, and the rest of my family and friends who have all supported me through some difficult years. I am very lucky to have so much love around me.

About the Author

Alyssa Dineen is a New York–based personal stylist and dating coach who has worked in the fashion industry for two decades.

Alyssa created the first-ever profile styling service for online daters, Style My Profile, from her personal experience with online dating and professional expertise in the fashion and design industry. As a working mom of two small children, she reentered the dating world after her divorce at age forty-one. She found the scene excruciating, a world ruled by apps catering to millennials, where people swiped through potential hookups faster than they could read a menu.

After living through the agonizing process, Alyssa ultimately met her boyfriend on Tinder. She's now helping online daters like herself transform their destinies by taking charge of their online dating profiles.